The Thing I've Played With The Most

Sound And Vision

The Thing I've Played With The Most

Prof. Anthon E. Darling, B.S.
Discusses His Favorite Instrument

David E. Walden

Sound And Vision

Table of Contents

SECTION III – OTHER

Foreword

Honestly, people, I can't remember when I've had a happier task to perform. As you all know, I'm sure, as Chairperson of the Registered Music Instructors Association of Chezlee Ont and Environs, I have many blessed events to attend and a host of delightful functions to perform. But when Anthon – our own, local. home grown, honey of a "maestro of the 88" – asked me to give my *"ALMA MATER"* – (to use the Latin, I think) – to this stunning masterpiece of a book, I was so thrilled I haven't sat down since.

Every single page of this titanic opus is full of it! Jam-packed with nuggets and gems about a thing I myself have played with all my life (and enjoyed immensely, I might add). Anthon and 'Thee' Maestro – Colli Albani, L.C.B.O. – are two of the most sought after men in our town and county. As well, they're often asked for speaking engagements at which they have titillated the minds of many a Chezlee maid and given them a lot to think about to boot.

What Professor Anthon E. Darling does for the piano in this book is not to be believed. He covers it top to bottom, left to right, back and forth until, by the end, there are absolutely no questions left. There are answers to questions in this book that I myself had not even thought to ask: and you all know how broad my coverage is! Anthon is omnisciently comprehensive in his approach to the piano and at times, as is so often the case when one is in the ecstatic heights of a learning experience, you just want to say, "Stop! Stop! Stop! I've had enough!!!!". But unwittingly, Anton plunges on to even greater revelations of pianistic truth until you are literally left in a wet mess of post-instruction exhaustion.

On top of it all, Anthon does it with that rollicking, feather-tickling, prodding, punching sense of humour that has left, I don't know how many of us, gasping for breath afterwards. You girls will be loosening your girdles and you men will be unbuckling your britches before you've got to the end of Chapter One. It's unlawful what that Darling fellow does to your funny bone.

Now as far as his metamorphosis is concerned – (I think that's the proper term but correct me if I'm wrong) – David E. Walden – the girls of the Chezlee Ont Parsnip and Arts Fest

Central Committee *and* ALL the members of the Chezlee Ont Registered Music Instructors Association (including both Clyde and Cyril) are his biggest fans. His gi-normous talent is only exceeded by his girth and pound per pound you always get your money's worth with Walden. Add to that, you're always guaranteed a blush and/or a giggle – both of which are needed in these desperate times.

Have I read this book? You betcha!

Would I buy it for an ailing friend, a fan of the piano, or a relative I actually like?

You bet your sweet rutabagus chips I would!

I am so delighted with it, that I have given it the "FULL MONTY" of the C.O.R.M.I.A. (including Clyde and Cyril) and the C.O.P.A.F.C.C. have unanimously declared the book "decree nisi"!

What more could be said? Honestly now, I ask you.

If you're reading this, it probably means you've purchased the book, so get to it! Enjoy! You'll never read anything like it and I mean that most sincerely.

Keyboard Blessings from Myself

(and the cats – both Bartholomew and Freddie)

Mabel May Squinnge, B.O.
Mar 1, 2001
Legion Hall Upper Room
(headquarters of the C.O.R.M.I.A.)

Preface:
"Yer on yer own, Anthon"

These, dear reader, are the very words I heard yelled at me from the caboose of the CNR train chugging its way out of Chezlee Ont, leading south to Deseronto and parts beyond. The voice delivering this ominous prognostication was that of my incandescent tutor and the fount of almost all my knowledge – namely Colli Albani, L.C.B.O., known fondly by me, Lucetta, some of the swine, a few ewes and a selected handful of conoscenti from Chezlee Ont's more prestigious literati as "The Maestro."

May I hasten to assure the reader that this shouted "Yer on your own" was by no means the bitter last word in some acrimonious disagreement between the Maestro and myself causing an irreconcilable bifurcation between us. Far from it! It was more like a "Bonne Chance" a "Best Wishes, Anthon" as the dear magister of the musicological realm wound his way off on a teaching assignment. Indeed, myself, Lucetta, one ewe and several of the Chezlee Ont culturati stood on the platform waving wildly and wishing our fondest farewells, not without a shed tear or two, but tinkled pink at the Maestro's good fortune.

Let me explain. As the result of a connection, through my distant cousin Mellverne Wynch, who gave a demonstrated lecture series on Music and the Book of Habbakuk to the southwestern Arkansas Chrysler small-parts distributors, our own Maestro – so dear to Lucetta and I here in Obscuria on the fringes of Chezlee Ont – has been asked to take up a Chair in Musicology at S.W.A.P.S. – the South Western Arkansas Peridontal School. The Chair was made possible by an endowment from the Chrysler small-parts distributors in appreciation for my distant cousin Mellverne's lecture series. Colli's assignment is to do a six-month research slash lecture intensive analyzing the dental effects of music in general. He was toying with a number of headings for the series when he left, although *Teeth and the Tonic Chord* was still his fave, while I still preferred the pithy *Mozart and Molars*. Lucetta had suggested a more shocking approach with the more controversial *Dissonance Produces Cavities,* but was voted down on the grounds of overt sensationalism.

While we all wish Colli well, his departure could not have been more inopportune. Our publisher, Geoffrey Savage – as a result of selling seven copies of our first book, *HOW TO STAY AWAKE DURING ANYBODY'S SECOND MOVEMENT*, and 19 copies of our second volume, *HOW TO LISTEN TO MODERN MUSIC WITHOUT EARPLUGS* – feels we're on a roll. "Let's ride the swell" said Geoff "and bring out the next one while things are still hot!"

This decision came the night Colli left for SWAPS and hence, his hastily shouted "Yer on your own ..."

Normally I would have felt bereft and inadequate had the third book in our series been on any other topic than the one titularly referred to as *The Thing I've Played With The Most*. As a matter of fact, I've played with it since the age of seven, I've taught a host of students to play with it, including Lucetta, whose fingerwork improved superbly, and it's the one area I do feel qualified to "be on my own" with – as it were. Namely – viz. – i.e. – specifically – the PIANO!

My indebtedness to Colli, however, remains a constant given and his emanuensistic presence will be felt throughout this present tome.

A Letter From Abroad: "Colli Here..."

Dear Anthon, Lucetta and the sheep, especially Tonya:
I am ensconced here in my musicological chair in Pickles Corners, the home of the South-Western Arkansas Peridontal School (or S.W.A.P.S. as they call it locally) and am reasonably content. Although I do miss the hustle and bustle – that flurry of intellectual and agricultural activity – so characteristic of dear old Obscuria, to say nothing of the urbane cornucopia of cultural credits offered in Chezlee Ont. And I do miss the Stoney Ripples. American beer is simply not the same. "Weak as water" as Alma Buttersleigh would put it, "weak as water!"

The students here are so laid back both in speech and demeanor that I find myself having to take copious amounts of Southern Whiskey prior to any encounter with them, either social or pedagogical, just to get down to their level of lethargy, apathy and bone-idle laziness. The excessive heat here does not justify their minimalist aims in life and studies and conversely I find it stimulating as I sit nightly, au naturelle, my feet in 2 buckets of cold water provided by my landlady Gnarla-Gene, and delve into my academic research.

SITTING AU NATURELLE WITH MY FEET IN TWO
BUCKETS OF WATER AT GNARLA GENE'S.

Incidentally, I have discovered that a Baroque through-bass line, if played vigourously enough, can necessitate a resetting of lower dentures and upper partial plates due to the regularity of its incessant rhythm and I've been doing experiments on the relationship between Scriabin's later works for piano and bleeding gums, but so far have come up with zilch.

I do hope the book is going well and do deeply regret not being there to poke and prod, pry and challenge, but such is the life of a research academe – a seeker of knowledge – a pioneer on the front lines of learning pushing the advancement of "what we know already" into those realms where "no mind has gone before." And if there's any mind more qualified for that job, I can think of no other than my humble self.

I may take a small detour en route home via Chattanooga and Poughkeepsie to visit 2 dear old colleagues of mine but will definitely be with you by asparagus harvest time.

Tell Lucetta not to burn the rutabaga chips and Tonya that I miss her.

In Musicological fondess

"Colli"

P.S. Make sure when you're discussing the various schools of piano playing – viz. The Anglo-Russian and the French – do not neglect to mention the Americans and their dreadfully abusive attitude toward the precious 88 black & whites. I heard a Texan here in Pickles Corners the other night who slapped and banged the ivories through a Brahms concerto in such a manner that it vacillated between blasphemy and obscenity. Imagine! Banging Brahms! And of course, he got a standing ovation. Here in America if you pronounce someone's name correctly you get an ovation. Oh well, it beats the stuff they've thrown at us, eh Anthon, in some of our more radical prèmiere /dèrriere performances of our more progressive/less accessible works. Standing ovations are easier to get off one's dress suit than smashed rutabaga stains, so the Americans do win on the grounds of cleanliness.

Anyway, do refer to their "martial art" attitude to piano playing and condemn it thoroughly. I want them to get a stinging literary reproof for what they've done to "the thing you've played with the most."

End of p.s.

No p.p.s.

A Gentle Reminder
(Just in Case It's Your First Time)

(although as this is my/our third volume you should really know us by now so I'll do it in point form so's the conoscenti won't get bored):

1. I'm Prof. Anthon E. Darling, B.S. a grad of B.S.U. in Chezlee Ont, where I reside in a suburban rural domicile called Obscuria with

2. Maestro Colli Albani, L.C.B.O., my mental mentor and musicological magister of international reknown (in these parts anyways), who is my sole source of cerebral inspiration and yet is a fine stall-mucker to boot.

3. Lucetta Teagarden makes up the last of our unique triangle and she provides us service in all the areas in which Colli and I are deficient and believe me they are not a few.

ANTHON   COLLI   LUCETTA
(he slipped under the table)

A word about Chezlee Ont:

While located in an agrarian/sylvan setting far removed from urban centres, Chezlee Ont nevertheless is a hotbed of cultural activities and the level of artistic merit at the annual Parsnip and Arts Fest is staggering. And just to prove this, let me quote some items from last year's P. & A. Fest program just to tempt and tantalize your aesthetic tastebuds:

Parsnip and Arts Special Presentations, Fall 1999

Rococonuts – a lecture by our own Maestro Colli Albani L.C.B.O. on Mozart's precursors who were a bit odd.

Elsie Maum's Studio recital – all of her bassoon students in concert performing a *Pervertimento for 13 Bassoons* by Ronnie Fludd.

An evening of *Fin-de-Siècle Ecstasy* – Miss Eustacia Krispley of Keady playing an all-Scriabin program transcribed for autoharp and she may dance as well. (Bring your binoculars if you remember last year's recital.)

Whistle up the Winds – a quintet for tin whistle, flute, clarinet, oboe, and used vacuun cleaner motor.

This is an interdisciplinary multi-media work involving certain movements as well as a complex score. Written by our Prof. Anthon E. Darling, the ending has certain surprise elements that players and audience get a real lift from.

So that's Chezlee Ont. And that's us and you'll get to know us better as you read on.

Dedication:
To Catherine

Beethoven taught
Czerny who taught
Leschetizky who taught
Hayunga Carmen who taught
Catherine Baird who taught
Me

Catherine taught me music through the piano. They were called piano lessons but they were so much more. The piano was the medium, the vehicle, the means by which I was taught so much about music and art and life and etc. etc. My indebtedness to her can never be repaid. Her victorious life in the midst of tragic circumstances, her knowledge of the greatest in music, her openess to the "latest" in music and her love and respect for humankind form one of the backbones of my existence both personally and artistically.

So thanks to you, Catherine, I play and play on.

May peace and Brahms and Bach surround you.

Ahem:
A matter of pronunciation

Some years ago, at a much earlier stage of my life here in
Chezlee Ont, two disastrous events occurred with devious simul-
taneousness that necessitated my leaving my natural surround-
ings and seeking my fortunes elsewhere. One of the horrid events
that occurred that particular spring was a dreadful drought that
dried up not only the flora and fauna of our agrarian community
but also the pockets of the formerly affluent farmers. No one
could afford to send their offspring or addlepated relatives for
musical instruction to the Maestro and me, and so an important
segment of our financial support dried up (like old Maude's teats
in winter). The second "horrid" event I cannot go into details
about in such an open and exposed publication as this book. But
it did involve certain rumors started, I am now convinced, by
Wilda Wroth and based on her disappointment that I had spurned
the amorous advances of her eldest daughter, Madge. The lengths
that some people will go to, when they (or those nearest and
dearest to them) have been "spurned in love" amazes me. Such
was the Wroth wrath, in this case, that the Maestro and I felt
the only course was for me to leave town "for a while" until matters had cooled down and Madge could find someone else to lav-
ish her large devotions upon. She did eventually lead Wilf Scraggs
down the matrimonial aisle, but their conjugal bliss was cut short
by Wilf's untimely passing on the night of their honeymoon in
Meaford Ont due to, so they said at the time, asthma. Anyway I
don't wish to veer from the point, which was to explain why I
went elsewhere some years ago.

As part of the motivation for going was our acutely impecu-
nious position (due to drought), I, of necessity, was forced to seek
employment, and one of the jobs I applied for was as an announcer
for the CBC. I was thrilled that I had gotten an audition with the
eminent national body and went for my interview with high hopes
and a certain gay abandon. Perhaps that was my hubris – my
fatal flaw. Too hopeful. Too gaily abandoned. For it was mere
moments later that I was out on the pavement again – unem-
ployed and red-cheeked embarrassed.

You see, it was a matter of ... ahem ... pronunciation.

I was asked to read the following script:

"...that was the final movement of the wonderful *Waldstein Sonata*, brilliantly played by the great pianist, Sviatoslov Richter."

Now, reading the above, dear reader, as you just have, you may leap to the conclusion that it was my pronunciation of Waldstein or Sviatoslov that caused them to unceremoniously end the interview and turf me back out on the streets. But you're wrong. My Waldstein and my Sviatoslov were immaculately perfect. It was my "pianist" that was off. Here's the problem: I had put the emphasis on the first syllable and slurred the second and third syllables into one monolithic lump.

The resultant sound "looked" like this:

"Pée-nsst!" with a definite emphasis on the "Pée."

The haughty drawl of the CBC employee in the sound booth as he thanked me for coming for the audition, was unmistakably dripping with sarcasm and disbelief. "Here at the CBC," he droned "we prefer to say "pee – án – ist" so that it does not get confused with a male body part." There were muffled chuckles from the back of the control room behind his voice and I stumbled as I fled from the studio to the crowded streets of Toronto. Humiliation and embarrassment, however, have forced me over the years to make sure I refer to someone who plays the piano as a pee-AN-ist – although I never again sought employment from the CBC.*

*Actually, that's not completely true. I've been paid (and cashed the cheques) for an interview about my last book, *HOW TO LISTEN TO MODERN MUSIC WITHOUT EARPLUGS.*

That was two years ago and although I call them semi-annually, I have not yet done the interview. Did they know about my earlier pronunciation blunder? Did fear of repetition prevent them? One wonders ... one wonders ...! **

** One also wonders exactly what's going on in the minds of those CBC executives when, in contrasting the playing styles of Rubenstein, Horowitz and Gould, they are thinking of male body parts. I say no more!

Chapter 1:
An Hysterical Glaze

Now, right off the top I want to say that the ABOVE title is NOT the CORRECT title of this chapter and how the printers got wind of the argument that occurred last Feb. at the Ox & Udder and changed it is a puzzlement to yours truly. The correct heading for this chapter should read "An Historical Gaze" and, as it implies, indicates a broad general overview of the piano and its ancestors over the centuries. However, as the printers have misrepresented my original manuscript (obviously having had their palms greased by that sly and wily F. T. Whigley), I feel it incumbent upon me to outline the details of the incident that led to the above titular misrepresentation. So do allow me this briefest of detours that, once cleared up, we can sally forth to the point without further peregrination and get on with it.

But first: I had been engaged in a bit of friendly intercourse with the sub-editor of the *Chezlee Sez* – Mr. F. T. Whigley – one Feb. eve when things got "out of hand" and, much to my great chagrin and embarrassment, eventually ended up in pushing. And worse, not only pushing but shoving as well. Such humiliating physical brutality as pushing and shoving still to this day brings crimson to my cheeks at its recollection.

The discussion had started off amicably enough but inevitably turned to a discussion of the arts – specifically music – and more specifically the massive contribution made to musical scholarship by our own musicological magister – viz. Maestro Colli Albani L.C.B.O.

And, in his absence, (Colli's – i.e.) there had been a great deal of discussion ABOUT the Maestro among the literati and conoscenti of Chezlee Ont. Not that it had ever degenerated into salacious and malicious gossip of any sort, but merely that objective viewpoint and critical analytical thinking that one CAN indulge in when the person you're discussing has been removed by death or a far-off posting (as was the case with Colli).

"F.T." and I were talking about "that Albani look" – that certain caste of that great mind's eyes of our beloved Colli that would occur late in the evening at the Ox & Udder when the discussion would move to the broader picture. I indicated to F.T. as I poured another flagon of Stoney Ripple Ale toward my glass, that this look I had dubbed *"An Historical Gaze"*

"You shee, F.T.," I slurred, "As Colli would move intellectually to "the broader picture and be searching for a terse and pithy summation of an entire century or a complete period (as in the Baroque was essentially a .... period), he would adopt the look of the HISTORICAL GAZE as he sifted through, in that grandiose cranial sieve, the details – the miniature – the macro collection of micro bites of socio-economic, political, cultural material in order to find that ONE WORD that would accurately epitomize the Baroque, the 19th century or whatever it was we had been talking about for hours and hours. And that's precisely when that HISTORICAL GAZE would come over Colli's entire face as he probed and pondered the library of his mind, collecting and collating the data that would soon be summarized by a single word, as in 'The Baroque was organized!' or some such pithy summation."

"Hogwash!" yelled F. T. Whigley as he slammed down his flagon of Stoney Ripple. "It is simply the result of the accumulative imbibation of Stoney Ripple that creates that ocular oddity. It's not an Historical Gaze at all – it's more an HYSTERICAL GLAZE – DUE TO BOOZE."

Needless to say, heated dialogue soon turned to puerile shouting, which then led to the aforementioned pushing and shoving. God knows what demonic levels we would have gone to in the end had not the kindly publican intervened with a quite brusque "Boys! Boys!" that immediately shook us to our senses. Recognizing the folly of our ways, we grudgingly shook hands and staggered into the night, each muttering his respective "GAZE" or "GLAZE" under his breath.

I think you can understand, dear patient reader, why I have taken this detour and why I became so upset as to actually push and shove when what was a look of deep searching was maligned and demeaned as a gaze of drunken stupor. I have a mind to tell the Maestro what F. T. said but I wouldn't stoop that low although the thought of the consequences is tempting.

"COULD WE GET ON WITH THE PIANO ?!!!#!!!?" I can virtually hear Colli's gruff and booming baritone all the way from Arkansas, and it does make me chuckle. But I obey, even in absentia.

To discuss the historical precedents of the modern piano, as we know it, we have to pare it down to its essential parts. I remember once when I myself was pared down to my essential parts – but that's another book.

The piano has

1. A KEYBOARD

and

2. A BUNCH OF STRINGS

3. Each key is attached to a HAMMER, which hits the string when the key is pressed.

COULD IT BE SIMPLER?

Honestly, now, I ask you...??

So, as we take our Historical Gaze, we are going to be searching in the murky darkness of antiquity for the predecessors of KEYBOARDS and STRINGS and HAMMERS and for this first chapter we will simply look for the earliest examples of each and leave it to the following chapter, viz.,i.e. *Blown, Clanged, Plucked and Hammered,* to see how the plethora of piano-like instruments developed over the ages to produce the masterpiece we know and love today.

To further elucidate the dimness of your minds, perhaps a diagram would be of assistance:

THE KEYBOARD	THE STRINGS	THE HAMMERS
organ	monochord	metal tangents
clavichord	psaltery	plectrum(s) or-a
virginal	harp	hammers
harpsichord	autoharp	spoons
piano		nails,
		odd bits of
		hardware

Now, this probably makes as much sense as that "Time for Planting Seeds" chart at Elmer Eebles Feed and Seed Emporium but please hold on to your academic britches because I'm about to clarify the mud!

Keyboards go back to the time of the Greeks, who had a water-operated organ called a HYDRAULIS with a loud penetrating sound. Around the 12th century, the idea of a KEYBOARD got wedded with the idea of strings being plucked or struck by the devices connected with the keys, until around 1700 the idea was born of a key attached to a hammer that then hits a string.

Please remember, dear truth searcher, that this chapter is one of general overview and it's the next chapter that will have all the nitty-gritty details in it. But, as Colli always says, you've got to have an overall idea of what something's all about before delving into the specific minutiae. Unless you're aware of the scope of the forest, the details of the trees, shrubs and leaves will leave you confused and uninformed.

So, in short, from the time of the Greeks, and before, there were keyboards (organs) and stringed instruments. Around the 12th century these started combining until in 1690 Panteleon Hebenstreit invented a large dulcimer (see next chapter) with hammers, which became known as the PANTALON. Bartolomeo Cristofori came along a bit later with better hammers so he usually gets the credit for inventing the piano.

And of course you all know why it's called the PIANO so I needn't mention the fact that:

Piano means soft (in Italian)
Forte means loud (in Italian)

And the PIANOFORTE (full name) was this NEW IN-STRUMENT that you could play both softly and loudly and shades in between.

I do apologize. I know every single one of you knew that, but I'm such an inveterate teacher and have been plagued with such thick-skulled numb-brained students over the years that I tend to reiterate a bit and "hit over the head" when I'm trying to get basics across.

However – enough now of overview. It's time to get our intellectual hands dirty and our academic hip-waders wet as we dive into that delicious sea of specifics that await us in the next chapter.

Brace yourselves! There's a brisk cranial wind about to blow!

Chapter 2:
Blown, Clanged, Plucked and Hammered

*

As you can see, dear reader, this space, normally reserved for an illustrative diagram, is BLANK! I had prepared the loveliest drawing embodying all four aspects of this purely historical chapter and the reactions ranged from "You've got to be kidding" to "...and you'll be tarred and feathered!" As a result, I have had to commence the current chapter sans that visual artistic prod to stimulate your minds in the areas I will be covering. Censorship is such a cruel and hurtful thing, damning the creative flow. However, I throw the challenge to you, dear reader, to let the four titular verbs describing the compass of this chapter reverberate through the annals of your collective minds and whet your intellectual appetite as we look at how the keyboard developed down through the centuries to the state it's in today.

Needless to say, the quadruple title of this chapter refers to the various METHODS USED to create sound in the piano's precursors, and we will look historically at them under those headings:

1) *THINGS THAT ARE BLOWN*

Now, right off the bat, I have to qualify this by stating that the earliest keyboard instruments – namely ORGANS – were not operated by WIND (as in AIR) but by WATER (as in wet). However, the good news is that while there may have been organs before, we have a date and an inventor of one kind that is the EARLIEST we have on record so it's a good jumping-off point. After this, the question of when and who did what becomes far fishier to figure out, so let's enjoy clarity whilst it reigns.

a. *THE HYDRAULIS*
Invented by an engineer called Ktesibios who lived in Alexandria around 250 BCE
b. The power source that pushed the air through the pipes of the organ was WATER
c. It had a loud, penetrating tone – noisy rather than musical
d. It was used in Rome chiefly as an accompaniment for popular entertainments like gladiatorial fights (c.f. also Hockey Nights at the Maple Leaf Gardens) and also for orgiastic cults. (Only those over 18 should look up orgiastic in your thesaurus.).
e. The Jews also had a hydraulis, which they called a MAGREPHA, and which they presumably used as part of their religious services as they tended not to have gladiatorial fights or certainly not anything orgiastic (although they liked garlic a lot!)
f. Apparently Nero performed on the HYDRAULIS himself during his gladiatorial half-time shows, and I think that's the whole story about the famous quote that Nero "fiddled with his organ" (namely the Hydraulis) while Rome burned. Doesn't that make sense?
g. It had 19 keys about eight inches long and two inches wide. They were actually called linguae (tongues), which were pulled out and pushed in: Draw your own conclusions.
And that pretty well covers it for the HYDRAULIS. And what happened next was that AIR replaced WATER as the power source for organs and bellows were used to pump air into the pipes to produce the sound. So now let's follow this air-operated organ through its highlights through the centuries:
a. *ORGANS THAT ARE BLOWN*
By the 4ᵗʰ century CE, this air-operated organ had become much bigger, with several men operating the bellows and several performers (men again, sorry ladies) used to operate the heavy large KEYS or SLIDES. (Again here, it's interesting to see the early connection with *Hockey Night in Canada,* as you would have two large groups of hot sweaty, well-biceped men working their buns off to produce a fleeting affect that was soon forgotten as soon as it stopped.)

b. St. Hieronymous (ca. 400) tells of an organ at Jerusalem that could be heard one mile away at the Mount of Olives. Talk about loud! They were obviously the ghetto blasters and car radios of the day that were difficult to talk above even back then.

c. They got even bigger! The monk Wulstan speaks of a MONSTER ORGAN in the 10th century at Winchester in England that had 26 bellows worked by 70 strong men. They "laboured with their arms, covered with perspiration, each inciting his companions to drive the wind up with all its strength, that the full-bosomed box may speak with its 400 pipes." Well, if there isn't fodder for the imagination in that description, you've got to be dead or comatose.

This monster organ was played by two (2) organists on two (2) keyboards, each of which consisted of twenty (20) slides – or what were later to become keys. And the effect of this monster organ? It was such that "everyone stops with his hand, his gaping ears, being in NO WISE ABLE TO DRAW NEAR AND BEAR THE SOUND!*

d. Organs got bigger and bigger! In 1429, the organ of the cathedral of Amiens had 2500 pipes

e. As well as monster organs, there were smaller ones:

i) portative – as the name implies, it was portable and handy, therefore, for parades and processions.

ii) positive – this was a medium-sized stationary organ (think "positive," as in "positioned") a.k.a. the Gothic organ.

f. By the 17th century, linguae and slides had become keys, foot pedals had been added, one to five manuals (keyboards) were stacked up, and ranks and ranks of pipes were used until you had pretty well the same kind of "church organ" that still exists today. Except for one major difference:

g. NOW electric motors force the wind through the pipes. Until Edison invented electricity, however, it was "the boys on the billows" and a lot of sweaty men that were needed to create all that wonderful organ music. So just remember that, all you hockey jocks that think music is such an effeminate and nancy-pancy frivolous thing. Where do you think the term "real men" comes from if it wasn't from those steamy organ blowers who pumped their butts off on church music for almost 2,000 years?

*I couldn't believe it when I read those words. Why the number of times I have been told by people that they CAN'T BEAR THE SOUND of my music ...

But enough of blowers. We move now to clangers:

2). *CLANGERS*

We move now from the earliest keyboard (the organ) to the earliest stringed keyboard instrument – namely the CLAVI-CHORD.

It dates from around the 12th century, when a keyboard was added to a harp-like instrument called the psalterium and put in a oblong wooden box – sometimes with legs, sometimes not (à table). The keys were attached to brass wedges on tangents. These metal bars hit or clanged the strings producing a soft, tinkly, delicate sound. It was the epitome of a subtle sound but capable of some dynamic variation, as in loud and soft and in between, similar to the piano.

The major problem was you had to be within about three feet of it, otherwise you'd think you'd gone deaf as a doornail. It therefore never really took off as a kind of concert or public performance instrument and remained as a domestic instrument, charming in its own right but so personal and private that a ménage-à-trois was about the biggest house it could play for.

By the 17th century it had pretty well gone bye-bye's everywhere except in Germany, where there is a slight tendency to hold on to things past their usefulness and, because of the generic nature of "keyboard" music during these early times, we don't know exactly the music that was written for it. So we'll leave it and move on to the harpsichord.

3. PLUCKERS

Just to ward off any misconceptions, I'm not referring here to the Wipple Girls (both Velveeta and Chesleigh), who do such a lovely job at the Free Range Hen House, where you can get plucked for about 50¢ a bird. Not bad, eh? and Vel and Ches do such a good job.

No I'm speaking of that great precursor of the piano – namely, i.e., viz., sic, the HARPSICHORD and its predecessors. And if we go right back to the earliest form of a plucker, we have to look at the HARP. And vis à vis harps, we're looking at ancient Mesopotamia, Babylon, Egypt and Israel as early as 3,000 BCE. King David of Israel plucked on a harp-like instrument in an attempt to calm down King Saul's excessive neuroses. Sadly for Saul, it didn't really work as an effective form of therapy, but David did get a reputation as a harp-playing healer.

To go through, century by century, from psaltery to zither, from kinnor and pektis to magadis, from kantele, gusli and rotta to cymbalum, from Fortnam and Mason's to Macy's and Gimble's, would take far too long and you can tell from the length of this sentence itself it would be boring as heck, so we'll leave it at that till the 14th century.

Around 1400 you have mention of a clavicymbalum. Around 1500, CROW QUILLS replaced the earliest leather plectra and from then on till 1800 there is a plethora of shapes and sizes, and a whole bunch of different names describing essentially what was the harpsichord. One of them was actually an upright box called the clavicytherium, but members of the

Anabaptist movement were dead set against it as they felt it might lead to stand-up sex, or worse yet, dancing, so it died out. They were also tough to get through the front door!

In comparison with the clavichord's weak and wussy sound, the harpsichord was a real Buffalo Bill's boomer. When them crow's quills plucked those strings, you could damn well hear it at the back of the hall. It also gave the performer visceral, tactile involvement in playing: When your finger pushes down a harpsichord key, you get a good bang for your buck that would turn off any namby-pamby pantywaist pansy. Why, after playing a vigorous three-part invention or a four-part fugue on a harpsichord, I can go out in the fields and furrow till dark, milk the cows, muck out the stalls and still feel as if I could fix the hole in the kitchen roof if it wasn't too dark out.

The thing about the harpsichord that was its limitation and the reason why the piano eventually, or rather quickly, replaced it was this: You could get very soft (*pp*), you could get soft (*p*) and you could get loud (*f*) but you couldn't get from one to the other gradually. You could, in other words, NOT get a crescendo ———————— or a diminuendo ———————— Now, the harpsichord works perfectly fine for the music that was written for it – and, as a matter of fact, probably much better on it than when you play music originally written for the harpsichord on the piano, although it can be done. If you ever get the chance, try to sit down at a harpsichord and bang out a tune. I tell you, and Lucetta will confirm it, it gets your testosterone going at a rate you haven't experienced since you were a kid. And I'm not kidding.

4. *THINGS THAT GET HAMMERED*

Honestly, it's impossible to discuss any serious topic nowadays without people misconstruing what you're saying. I announced the above heading as the title for my spring lectures to the Nasturtium Dahlia and Pansy Society as part of their historical series *Spring Forward, Let's Look Back!* Anyway, the comments were quite uncalled for and while the Maestro does de temps en temps have to quiet the excessive raging of his gargantuan intellect with a thimbleful of Stoney Ripple, and I, purely out of social companionship, will join him in a soupçon sip of the same, neither of us has ever been hammered, to the best of my recollection. Although there is one week in November of '95 that does not come to mind with complete clarity. But that's not the purpose of this section, to which I now return:

Here again we find ourselves way way back in the ancient worlds of Assyria and Persia with a harp-like instrument (psaltery) called a DULCIMER that, instead of being plucked with the fingers or a plectrum, is actually banged by SMALL HAMMERS held in the hand.

Now, the dulcimer (also called a zither) wandered down the annals of time until around 1690, when a man by the name of Pantaleon Hebenstreit invented a large dulcimer that had 185 strings and was played by means of two small hammers. Hebenstreit (or Pantaleon, as he was known to his friends) toured all over Europe as a virtuoso performer on his instrument and it became known as the PANTALON (without the 'E' or sometimes with it). In 1767 an English guy by the name of George Nölli (or Noel if you're English) gave a concert on a similar instrument with 276 strings. His two little hammers must have been kept busy trying to bang out a tune on 276 strings.

However, as good as old Pantaleon and George were, they don't get the credit for inventing the piano. No, it was Bartolomeo Cristofori, who in 1709 developed a hammer mechanism making it possible to play soft, soft to loud and loud on a harpsichord-like instrument – AND SO THE PIANO-FORTE WAS BORN!

piano:	soft
forte:	loud
together:	the soft/loud
shortened to:	the soft
or:	the PIANO

There was still a lot of perfecting to be done and here are some of the greats in that process:

Gottfried Silbermann

- in the textbook it says he had a *hopper* or an escapement. I think this means he *did* a *hopper* and *made* an *escapement*. Perhaps some creditors were after him.

Johann Andreas Stein

- reintroduced Silbermann's hopper and developed what was to become known as GERMAN ACTION and I'll leave that there as it is. It was also called the VIENNESE ACTION and again, according to the sources, "it delighted Mozart when he visited Stein's workshop in 1777." Now that, I'm not touching with a 10-ft. Pole, or a 10-ft. German or even a 5-ft. 4-in.Viennese.

Johann Andreas Streicher
- Stein's son-in-law, so no wonder he gets credited with making a contribution, although his was described as elegant in appearance and sound with a very light action.

John Broadwood
- in England, developed heavier structure (typically English! Ever eaten a Mowbrey Pie???), greater tension (ibid.) and two pedals and his action became known as ENGLISH ACTION, which was heavier than the Viennese but more expressive and dynamic.

A. Babcock
- Boston, 1825, the first full cast-iron frame for a piano

Sebastien Érard
- Paris, 1821 – invented double escapement (sounds like getting out of jail twice!)
- first Babcock, then Steinway & Sons of New York, developed cross-stringing. Notice this is not cross-dressing but cross-stringing. And before you start thinking any nasty thoughts, go to a grand piano – or any piano, for that matter – and look inside it. You'll understand in a flash what is meant by cross-stringing.

And you know, that's about it!

The PIANO remains a stringed instrument covering seven octaves (and a bit), and the strings are struck by hammers put in motion from keys by means of connecting mechanisms known as the ACTION! Scientifically it's classified as a ZITHER and has three foot pedals:

1. Damper – takes felt dampers OFF the keys and lets them keep ringing after the fingers have left the keys
2. Sostenuto – takes dampers OFF the keys that are depressed ONLY when you put it down
3. Soft Pedal – makes the sound softer by:
a) moving hammers closer on upright pianos
b) shifting hammers over on a grand piano so they hit one string (una corda) instead of three strings (tre corde)

And basically that's it! And as the sun has gone down on the yardarm, I'm off to the Ox & Udder for an ale and egg and a chat with Shirley from the Cheese Factory.

31

Chapter 3:
The Only Place to SEE Music

As the ancient Chinese philosopher Confucius said: "A picture is worth a thousand words," *or* as Colli used to say – late of an evening in asparagus stalk- shredding season when, exhausted from our arduous labours, we would lie back on the bristley stumps, and knock back a few Stoney Ripples, discussing various aspects of the history of music – "If you can draw a picture, Anthon, it saves you yards of verbal dribble." And that's what I've decided to do, as verbal dribble can be so annoying (particularly yards of it).

Now, before we discuss the topic of this chapter – namely, viz., i.e., that THE KEYBOARD IS THE ONLY PLACE TO (actually) SEE MUSIC, may I quote an interjected aside of our dear Lucetta Teagarden when, upon hearing Colli and I discussing where the best place to see music was, suddenly turned from her rutabaga chip slicing and said, somewhat haughtily, "I thought music was to be heard and not seen!"

Well, the torrent of invectives that flew from the Maestro's lips was of such magnitude and foulness that Lucetta's rutabaga chips oxidized on the spot and one of the ewes had a miscarriage. Colli later apologized to Lucetta and bought her a very large cheddar from Ingersoll and a bottle of herbalized salad dressing that he himself was quite fond of and all, or certainly most, was forgiven.

The boiled-down point of what the Maestro spewed that night was MUSIC MUST BE SEEN TO BE UNDERSTOOD.

Lucetta, having just typed the above section, has accused me of suffering from senilia dementia and getting it all wrong. Apparently Colli and I that night were discussing which were the best of Brahms' piano sonatas and Lucetta's comment was:
"I thought the third was obscene!"

And furthermore it wasn't a cheddar from Ingersoll but head cheese from Hanover that was given to placate the ruffled Teagarden feathers.

With Lucetta's help, I've been able to reconstruct and so I re-commence this chapter.

I must confess, right off the top, that the credit for this entire chapter does go to the Maestro himself and, specifically, one cold bitter night in Farch when Colli and I were in heated musicological debate at one of the back tables of the Ox & Udder.

Stoney Ripples had flowed consistently throughout our Socratic intercourse from tankard to stein to gullet and we were rapidly approaching last call, as well as rather complete inebriation. We had been arguing about the relative merits of possessing perfect pitch, and were mapping out a lecture on same, which we were booked to deliver at the spring meeting of the Cauliflower and Clematis Club of Bognor.

Just at the point when we were shouting quite loudly at each other "Perfect Pitch – Boon!" and "Perfect Pitch – Bane!" the landlord's telephone rang. The sudden intrusion of the Bell tone so startled us that the Maestro immediately burst out with: "I hear a B-flat!!!"

And then, as a complete non sequitur, and probably due to the massive number of S. Ripples I had consumed, I shouted back sarcastically: "Yes, but can you SEE it?" chuckling at my own witty riposte.

In a flash, that titanic mind thundered back:

"Yes, Anthon, I can! At the keyboard! The ONLY place to SEE Music!"

And he banged his stein down so heavily on the table that its (the table's) spindly legs collapsed, our Stoney Ripples spilled everywhere and the landlord got quite nasty, as it had been the third table that week that had "fallen" due to an emphasized point by the Maestro.

The repercussions, intellectually, however, of that brilliant observation have continued to filter down and influence our thinking and its ramifications affect us to the present day.

Let me illustrate:
Here's a singer
singing B-flat:

A SINGER SINGING Bb

Can you tell it's a B-flat? No!
Here's a violinist playing a B-flat? No!

Here's a trumpet tooting a B-flat:

Can you tell it's a B-flat? No!
I could go on and on throughout the entire range of instruments and the answer would still be the same – namely – NO!
BUT, here's a pianist playing B-flat:

Can you tell it's a B-flat?
YES! YOU CAN SEE IT'S A B-FLAT RIGHT THERE BEFORE YOUR EYES!
The keyboard, whether organ, harpsichord, piano, or synthesizer, is the only place where you can actually see music!

And furthermore, with the piano covering seven octaves (and a bit), it has the broadest biggest range of notes of any other instrument so not only can you

SEE MUSIC AT THE PIANO, you can

SEE MORE MUSIC AT THE PIANO than anywhere else.

Now, there are those, dear reader, who would be content to leave you here, reveling in the wonder of this discovery, but I can hear the Maestro's voice, quietly chiding saying: "Anthon ... give them the whole picture ... not everything is as it seems ... be a teacher! ... tell all!

And so I must obey! (Amazing, isn't it, that even though our dear Colli is absent in the flesh, his spirit and mind penetrate the very environs of Obscuria and, whether under the influence or not, his influence seeps into our lives just like bug-water, when it rains, seeps into our fruit cellar and ruins Lucetta's rutabaga chips supply and upsets her terribly.

Now, the point that I was making was ... ... ah yes ... tell all! And here it is in a nutshell. Perhaps a nitty-gritty detail but a profound one that will sky-rocket through your brains and repercuss for days.

Here's a section of KEYBOARD

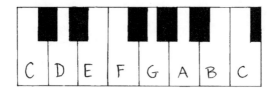

What a wonderful *view* of an octave of music! No where else can you *see* it like that! Wow!

HOWEVER, one little slight adjustment or qualification has to be made:

THE WHITE KEYS ARE THE SAME WIDTH!

The distance from C to D, D to E, E to F, *LOOKS* AS IF IT WOULD BE THE SAME.

BUT, here's where you have to gird your intellectual loins and fasten your seat belts because, in truth, the AURAL DISTANCE is *NOT* ALL THE SAME.

Let me show you:

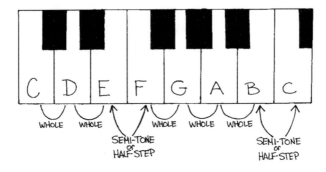

Do you "SEE" it???

From E to F and from B to C is only HALF the distance that is between the other notes.

"WHY WHY WHY?" I can hear rebounding through the empty corridors of your minds.

The answer is simple and it's this:

Keyboards developed over long periods of time – yea verily, centuries – and long before they knew about whole steps and half steps. And once things have become established practice, it's hard to change them even when you know better. (How true that is of life, as well as of musical notation and instrument construction.)

So while it *LOOKS* as if the distance from E to F is the SAME, as the distance from C to D , D to E, F to G, G to A, and A to B, it's not! It's only *half* the distance – and the same is true for B to C.

However, apart from that one visual anomaly, the KEYBOARD shows us wonderfully what MUSIC LOOKS like and that's one of the reasons why the piano is soooooo popular and I think that deserves a new chapter. And so ...

Chapter 4:
Shocking Revelations as
to why the PIANO is SOOOO Popular

Those of you who have read this chapter heading and are here because of the words "Shocking..." and "Popular" should rather go to your local supermarket and buy the *National Enquirer* or its equivalent here in Chezlee Ont, *"The Out-House Mirror."* This is a serious chapter involving much pedagogical content and therefore should be tackled only by the brave and dauntless. If you have the slightest bit of "daunt'" you'd best go on to the next chapter because we're about to delve into the VERY NATURE OF MUSIC ITSELF and make some SWEEPING GENERALIZATIONS. So, for those of you still with us ... we carry on!

In general (and I mean VERY general) there are three (3) kinds of MUSIC – both historically and currently – and they are:

1. A SINGLE MELODY,
represented thusly:

and called monophonic music.

2. MUSIC that COMBINES MELODIES,
represented thusly:

and called polyphonic music.

3. MUSIC that combines a MELODY with a HARMONIC ACCOMPANIMENT,
represented thusly:

and called homophonic music.

Now just take a moment, reread the above and let it digest in the stomach and bowels of your minds, so that we can sail forth knowingly.

Here are the *"Shocking Revelations"*

1. Almost every instrument, by itself, or any singer, by him or herself, *can* play a SINGLE MELODIC LINE.

2. *Only* a GROUP of instruments or a GROUP of musicians can play POLYPHONIC MUSIC: i.e music that combines more than one melody.

3. *Only* a GROUP of instruments or a GROUP of musicians can play HOMOPHONIC music – i.e. music that combines a melody with some sort of harmonic accompaniment.

> BUT
>
> *One* person at the PIANO (and KEYBOARD instruments in general)
>
> CAN play a single melody line (monophonic).
>
> CAN play music consisting of a number of melodies (polyphonic).
>
> CAN play music consisting of a melody with an harmonic accompaniment (homophonic).

DO YOU SEE THE SHOCKING REVELATION THAT THESE FACTS PRESENT US WITH?

The reason the piano has been and is Sooooooooo Popular is that a pianist can:

1. play music specifically written for the piano

2. play music written for choirs or groups of instruments, either polyphonic or homophonic.

Hence, keyboard instruments were used to give people an idea of all different kinds of music, from symphonies and operas to hymns and dances! This is a good thing, as Martha Stewart would say.

Suppose you played the flute: You could play only a single melody line (monophony) unless you joined together with a whole bunch of other instrumentalists and played polyphonic or homophonic music together.

Suppose you are a single tenor singer: You could sing only a single line (monophony) of music, unless you joined together with other men and women and formed a choir and then *together* you could sing polyphonic or homophonic music.

But a pianist herself or himself can sit down at that piano bench (or sturdy chair) all alone and play:
- a piano transcription of an entire symphony or concerto
- a piano transcription of a mighty choral work for choir and organ
- a piano transcription of a great aria from an opera
- a piano transcription of a dance piece from a ballet.

In other words, ANY or ALL MUSIC *can* be transcribed for the piano and played by one (1) person, and give you a good idea how the whole thing sounds.

Needless to say, in an age before

Record players

Tapes

CDs

Etc.

When the ONLY music you EVER heard was LIVE music, A KEYBOARD INSTRUMENT was the only and best way to hear all sorts and kinds of music and that's why it became soooooo popular.

There are, therefore, two (2) kinds of music written for the keyboard (piano, etc.):

1. Music written specifically for the PIANO

2. Music transcribed from other sources, instrumental, vocal, etc, whereby you could "get an idea" of what it sounds like "on the piano."

As music moved from the courts and palaces out into the homes of the upper, then middle and even the lower classes, so did the piano or its historical equivalent. Eaton's catalogue at the turn of the last century, circa 1900, advertised tons of pianos, all shapes, sizes and prices, for every home.

The piano has been, in the past, at any rate, the way most people heard MUSIC. Nowadays, because of advances in recorded music, it has settled down to being primarily just a piano, playing music written specifically for it, 'cause you can buy a CD of just about any piece of music written by anybody in the world, anytime, anywhere. So most homes NOW have a CD player, or an equivalent. But not every home has a piano anymore and, consequently, pianists are harder to find than they used to be.

So, in conclusion, as well as being the only place where you can SEE music, the piano is the only instrument that can play ALL DIFFERENT kinds of music!

No wonder it was/is sooooo popular*

*and I'm not just saying that because I'm a pianist and piano teacher but because it's the truth. And while the guitar has become immensely popular, it *cannot* (and I hope the McWhurtzer boy is listening!), I repeat, *cannot* equate with the piano in terms of what it can do.

An interjection:
The REASON most students HATE Clara Shumann

I always remember Ellveema Crumleigh in my Grade 3 class. Ellveema was one of those extremely intelligent and gifted persons who, quite early on in life, knew she was brighter than most of her peers, had a photographic memory and was a tattletale. If the teacher asked, "Is there anyone...?" Ellveema's hand would shoot right up and her obnoxious "ME ME ME!" would ring through the class before any of the rest of us had had time to hear the rest of the question. Thus Ellveema was hated passionately by pretty well everybody in the class because there *were* some times when you *did* know the answer to the teacher's question and you wanted at least a chance to answer it. Also there were certain things in your life that you preferred were not blabbed about all over Chezlee Ont.

I never met Clara Schumann, but in many respects, she's always reminded me of Ellveema. She was the wife of the famous composer/concert pianist Robert Schumann, who eventually went a little cuckoo and had to be put in an asylum. The reason, "THEY SAY," he went nuts, was that he'd invented a device to strengthen and stretch his fingers so he could play louder and faster. However the thing backfired on him and wrecked his fingers so completely that his concert career was over. "SO THEY SAY." However (and perhaps it's the horrid memory of that annoying Ellveema Crumleigh niggling on my historical brain cells), ...but ... I wonder (and I say this purely speculatively), did Clara – with her "anything you can do, I can do better" attitude – have something to do with driving her husband el nutso? Call me crazy, call me old-fashioned, but I think there could be some truth here in my postulations. Perfectionists are difficult to live with, and I know that so well from my own experience – and I don't wish to digress here, but as the Maestro is not here to yell at me to "get back to Clara," I am going to veer slightly from that Clara-ine track and make a hitherto unknown revelation.

In my youth, shortly after graduating from B.S.U. in Chezlee Ont, I roomed for a brief period of time with a certain aforementioned Mr. G.D. Phineas in rather small and cramped quarters above the Creamery just off Main Street. And may I say here in print that living with an anal-retentive, obsessive-compulsive, everything-at-right-angles, neurotic perfectionist almost drove me "up the hill" *

How often during those months-that-seemed-like-years did I say things like:

a) I might as well have married Ellveema Crumleigh – and/or

b) You're a right Clara, aren't you? (hence, ergo, ibid, sic, Clara Schumann, aforementioned).

So, to return to the point, from my personal experience with that particular personality type, I think Clara was semi-responsible for sending Bob to the nuthouse. I know I would have ended "up the hill," had I not been rescued by running into our dear Colli at the Ox & Udder one bitter night in the month of March and as a result soon left G.D. to live here in Obscuria with Lucetta and the Maestro.

The other thing I thought was a bit hard-hearted-Hannah-ish of Clara was this: Johannes Brahms had been desperately in love with Clara for years. Bob (as in Robert Schumann) went nuts and died young. Clara could have married Brahms and given him (and her) a lot of marital bliss instead of the widow's weeds for her and a lot of suppressed desires for Brahms. I give him the credit 'cause he never got bitter and turned out to be a nice little old man who gave candies to kids as he went out walking around Vienna.

Clara, on the other hand, was making fame and fortune as a travelling concert pianist playing her late husband's music plus a piece or two of her own, as she also fancied herself a composer. And every time she played, because she had a pho-tographic memory, SHE NEVER USED THE MUSIC – AND THAT'S WHY STUDENTS HATE HER SO MUCH.

* "up the hill" is a local expression here in Chezlee Ont, as the General Marine and Cattle Hospital with the Virma Eustatch Mental Wing is up on the east hill behind the abattoir. Virma was a local matron of generous means who went quite odd at the end but left her money to the G.M.&C.H. Hence, anyone who had to be incarcerated for a while, having veered off the straight and narrow path of sanity, was said to be "up the hill." It is a nice way of putting it, isn't it, without being specific or unkind?

Before Clara Schumann:
- all keyboard players used the music and it was O.K.
Clara Schumann:
- because she was such a little smartypants, she never
played using the music.

THE YOUNG CLARA SCHUMANN <u>NOT</u>
USING MUSIC!!!

After Clara Schumann:
- every single pianist from kiddies recitals to the concert
stage HAS TO PLAY FROM MEMORY. And if that hasn't
wrecked the nerves and careers of a lot of good players, then I
don't know what has. And as a teacher, the angst I've had to go
through teaching my students how to memorize – giving them
the four-step method of memorization:
DIGITAL
VISUAL
AURAL and
STRUCTURAL
and keeping more than my fingers crossed while the little buggers were stumbling through a sonatina and habitually getting
lost in bar 33 ...Honestly, I tell you, it's enough to drive a person to the Ox & Udder for more than a quick Stoney Ripple
Ale!

And, to be honest with you, I've told my students it's all
Clara's fault and we've actually formed little "We Hate Clara"

clubs and have meetings where we play all sorts of pieces US-ING THE MUSIC and making rude raspberry-like sounds at the end of major (and minor) cadences as we look proudly at the music in front of us.

The other good thing resulting from this ANTI-CLARA movement is the re-employment of those wonderful assistants: THE PAGE TURNERS.

I myself now will perform only USING the music and have had the great privilege of working with a number of wonderful page turners, to whit:

Frances Fillmore (except when she's had garlic)

Wilber Waugh (unless he's been drinking)

And the McNullought boy, except that he sometimes dribbles.

So there you have it, in something more than a nutshell, why Clara Schumann has been the cause of so much nerve-racking anxiety among so many would-be and/or wannabe pianists down through the ages since her time.

Why, I myself could have had a stunning international concert career if I'd been allowed to use the music!

Do you see what you've done, Clara???

Chapter 5:
Loosey Goosey – Keyboard Music pre-1700

TED WETSTONE,,,,,,,,,M or F?

Keyboard music prior to 1700 always reminds me of one of Chezlee Ont's most interesting characters – namely, Ted Wetstone. I don't know whether it strikes you the same way, but when I look at an Elizabethan "dompe" or a French "galliard" or "gallope" or a German "tedesca," I'm always put in mind of Chezlee's Ted Wetstone.

The reason for this, of course, for those of you who might not have known Ted, was that no one – and I mean NO ONE – in Chezlee Ont. or its environs knew whether Ted was a man or a woman. Now, let me rush to assure you, dear reader, that there is absolutely *no* judgmentalism in our uncertainty as to Ted's gender. It did not matter one iota to anyone. It was merely idle curiousity and the subject of discreet debate whilst mating bulls and cows or assisting with an ewe's birth. The general consensus of opinion was the truth would only be ascertained posthumously and so we lived with and enjoyed Ted's bubbly if enigmatic personality whoever or rather whatever he or she was.

Well, pre-1700, keyboard music is much like Ted Wetstone. You can't really tell what instrument it was written for. In some cases, it looks like it could have been sung or played by any number of keyboard instruments. Who knows? It could go many ways. Just like Ted.

And to be honest, if the Maestro had had his own way, this chapter would not have been written. He is such a black-and-white scholar, such a seeker of the truth regardless of the cost, that any areas of learning that are PERMANENTLY GREY drive Colli quite right round the bend. Anything that can "go either way" is utterly abhorrent to him and so, when I mentioned my desire to write a chapter on Keyboard Music prior to 1750, he went ballistic, took potshots at a peafowl lurking behind the asparagus patch and shouted "Why bother? Ya can't tell what's what or who's who!" and stomped off toward the woods following a flurry of peafowl feathers.

And that's true! With respect to keyboard music before 1750, you cannot really tell which keyboard instrument the music was written for. However, in spite of this flopsy-mopsy, loosey-goosey state of affairs, I feel strongly the importance of telling you as much as I can and hope that this book gets to the publishers before Colli gets back from S.W.A.P.S. and rips it out. (Oh, he can be such a strident man at times when he thinks he's in the right – but he is wonderful and I do hold him in such high regard that his little peccadillos are easily forgivable.)

An Inner Preface!

The earliest keyboard music that we know about was obviously for the organ, as it predates the piano and its precursors by centuries. But, as the purvue of my survey is the piano, I shall not enter into a detailed discussion of the music written for organ.

I will not discuss the earliest examples, from what is called the Robertsbridge Codex of motets and estampies (dances), or the preludes of the Ileborgh tablatures. Nothing will be said of the Buxheim organ book of 1470 with its Burgundian chansons.

References will not be made to the fact that from these early beginnings, by 1750, there were three national schools of organ playing and composition, namely French, German and Italian, and organ music had reached the dizzying heights of the great Johann Sebastian Bach, above which heights few have sailed higher since! No, I am resolved not to mention any of this!

As we do look at the music of the more specific precursors of the piano, we find that here, too, they fall into national schools – namely English, Dutch, German, Italian and French – and we will now discuss them in that order.

The English

Members of this school, which started during the reign of Queen Elizabeth I, were called the "English Virginalists" because the primary keyboard instrument of this period, other than the organ, was called the VIRGINAL. Now, of course, right off the bat we have to deal with all the risqué implications as to why it was called a virginal and why those who played it were called virginalists.

There are a few limp theories blowing around in musicological circles that say it had to do with the "virgin" Queen, Elizabeth I, who was one (supposedly) and played one (definitely), or that it came from the Latin word VIRGA, meaning rod or jack, referring to early notes (neumes) used for writing music. Well, I think both theories are "Weak as water," as Velma Squires always said about the dandelion wine Lucetta made for the annual church bizarre (and it was, too!).

No, the meaning is obvious and I think you'll agree, dear reader. Young women, before finding the joys and ecstasies of marital, and even a bit of premarital sex, had to find something to play with and what better thing than a keyboard?

Once married, however, their conjugal duties as well as domestic responsibilities, even if it was telling the servants what to do, were so onerous that little to no time was left for such idle pleasures as fooling around on the keyboard. Call me old-fashioned, call me simplistic, but I think they were called virginals because they were played primarily by young virgin women. The men who wrote the music for them and played them themselves were obviously not virgins, as most of them had kids, but musicians slash composers have always been different anyways, and continue to be so.

Who were these famous English Virginalists? Here's a list, with asterisks for the real biggies:

William Byrd *
Thomas Morley
Peter Philips
Giles Farnaby
John Bull *
Thomas Weekes
Orlando Gibbons *

And there you have it, with Byrd, Bull and Gibbons the greats. They wrote mainly dances, variations, preludes, fantasies and a host of other virginal ditties as well as transpositions of madrigals. And here you have an early example of the importance and popularity of the keyboard instrument because you could take a madrigal – a vocal piece written for three, four, five or more voices – and transcribe it to be played by one virginalist. And in an age long before radios, records or the CBC, the keyboard was a way to hear music you couldn't have heard otherwise.

One of the biggest collections of virginal music is called the *Fitzwilliam Virginal Book,* which contains 297 compositions by the whole pack of virginal composers. And for some reason after the virginalists died off, that was 'it' for English keyboard music. Some even say that, after the great music of the Elizabethan period (vocal as well as virginal), that was 'it' for great English music, with the exception of Henry Purcell who died young in 1695, until Elgar and Holst came along. Whether that's true or not, there are not a lot of keyboardists to talk about after Elizabeth I.

Cromwell killed a lot of artistic endeavours during his short reign and probably put the virgin and the virginalists off so that they never recovered. Mind you, virgins do have a habit of dying out as a breed if they remain that way too long, so maybe it was the name that eventually killed the school.

The Dutch (this won't take very long)

Bull and other virginalists nipped over to the Netherlands and produced what is described in some textbooks as "cross-fertilization." Now, I'm telling you right off the top I'm not going to get involved in any of that nonsense. However, the dominating Dutchman of this early period was Jan Pieterszoon Sweelinck. Most of his work was for the organ and he founded the northern Germanic school of organ playing whose eventual graduate was J.S. Bach himself and that's about it for the Dutch. (See, I told you it wouldn't take long.)

The German

Here again we are dealing with a preponderance of organ music and, thanks to one of the early composers – viz. Samuel Scheidt (1587-1654), who really established the use of foot pedals – you could begin to tell the differences between organ music and music for harpsichord. Organ music had three staves (one for Right Hand, one for Left Hand, one for Foot Pedals), whereas harpsichord music had only two staves, one for each of the hands – although, even here, the music could be played on the manuals of an organ as easily as on a harpsichord. Confusing, isn't it? These situations can go either way. But that's the way it was.

Let me throw at you a list of the biggies of German Keyboard Music. Needless to say, it will be Bach-less because ol' J.S. Bach gets a complete chapter to himself. Now, I'm not going to give you dates 'cause you won't remember them anyways, so what's the point? Look 'em up if you have to. Here's the list of G.B.'s (German Biggies):

Samuel Scheidt
Dietrich Buxtehude
Johann Kaspar Ferdinand Fisher (one composer only)
Johann Jacob Froberger
Johann Kerll
Georg Böhm
Johann Pachelbel
Johann Kuhnau
Georg Philip Telemann

Some interesting things to notice about the above:

i. notice the shortage of first names available in Germany during this period

ii. Pachelbel IS the author of Pachelbel's canon, and if I hear that repetitive piece of junk one more time on classical radio I'll throw up

iii. Kuhnau wrote a set of keyboard pieces called *Musical Representations of some Bible Stories* (1700), including names like "Saul cured by David's musicmaking" and "The grave sickness of Hezekiah and his recovery." I've often wanted to hear Hezekiah's grave sickness section but haven't been able to find the score.

I once wrote a similar piece for piano during a bad bout of gastroenteritis, but it never gained much popularity with the public.

That about covers it for the German school.

The Italian

When we speak of Italy during this period, there really

are two names but three composers. "What kind of an enigmatic conundrum is this?" you may well ask. Well, as Desi would
say, "Let me 'splain!"

Here are the three Italian biggies:

Girolamo Frescobaldi

Alessandro Scarlatti (the father)

Domenico Scarlatti (the son)

Now, while Frescobaldi was foundational, and Scarlatti –
the dad – was significant, it was the son, Domenico, who was
truly great, particularly with respect to keyboard music, and
he wrote over 600 sonatas and pieces for harpsichord.

And these pieces were unmistakably for harpsichord and
nothing else and remain as keyboard gems that have easily been
translated to the pianoforte idiom and remain "popular" to this
day.

At this juncture, I would encourage you to listen to some
(Domenico) Scarlatti. It's a wonderful place to start when ex-
ploring keyboard music and, like the difference between fet-
tuccine alfredo and bratwurst mit knoedles, Scarlatti is much
lighter and easier to digest than the Germans, even the great
one (not Gretzky!).

The French

Speaking of lighter than the Germans, we now look at the
French Clavecinistes. Clavecin was the French word for harpsichord and there obviously were no virgins in France, so that
word never came into play. The words that *do* come into play
when talking about the French and their harpsichord music
are more like the following:

ornamental

light

delicate

style brisé

elegant

whimsical

etc.

Get the picture?

The biggest names among French Clavecinistes were:

Jacques Champion de Chambonnières (founding father)

Louis Couperin & Jean Henri d'Anglebert

(both pupils of Chambonnières) and

François Couperin (nephew of Louis) and the most famous! François published 27 suites of harpsichord music, with some suites containing up to 20 pieces. He also wrote a text-book on how to play the harpsichord called *L'art de toucher le clavecin*. In it, as well as helpful hints as to how to perform the music of his period, he gives directions on how to sit at a harp-sichord, wearing a light smile for the assembled company. Now, I don't care how big your smile is, if that's all you're wearing whilst seated at the harpsichord, it's bound to be distracting, particularly for those in the front row who can see! No wonder the French get the reputation they have, and historically they certainly started early at developing it!

The last French biggie, and a contemporary of Bach, was Jean Philippe Rameau. He was a real lulu (not to be confused with his rival Lully) and was always getting into scraps, argu-ments and controversy. One of his frays was actually called the War of Buffoons. But buffoon he was not. He wrote a trea-tise on harmony called *Le Traite de l'harmonie* that was a foundational theoretical and compositional cornerstone. His keyboard music required virtuoso technique, but he preferred, if the truth be known, to write dramatic operas. If you've not heard a Rameau (or a Couperin), now's a good time to start.

And, while we've been sniffing around his edges, nudging his extremities, hinting at his greatness and declaring him tops, it's time we took a look at the Great One – and no, I still don't mean Gretsky!

Chapter 6:
The GREAT ONE
(and I'm not talkin' hockey!) et al.

First of all let me make it clear!
This fool is NOT rushing in
But also
This Angel is NOT fearing to tread!
"How can a humble piano teacher from Chezlee Ont dare to tackle a subject as mighty as Johann Sebastian Bach?" I can hear e'en now ringing from the rafters and particularly from those pedantic critics at B.S.U.

"Well, why not?" I would boldly reply and I know Colli would back me up in this endeavor (although I do miss his detailed and comprehensive knowledge of all music, musicians and eras, but we'll plug on.)

BACH'S BRAIN!

Colli and I once had the privilege of driving in the old buckboard down to Squallor's Corners, just south of Shivering ington to hear a lecture by the local veterinarian, Dr. T. Widgett, on the size of Bach's brain. He was incidentally an avid fan of the classical music realm and he himself, between birthing calves and deworming sows, would spend hours playing the works of Bach on an old pump organ he'd hooked up to a vacuum cleaner motor so he didn't have to pump.

Doc Widgett had taken calipers to a picture of Bach painted during his lifetime (Bach's, that is). Now, the old Doc knew brains. In his veterinary practice, he had done a pile of posthumous diddling around with brains of his ex-clients. And if the artist who drew the portrait of J.S. Bach was a good one and not wall-eyed or short-sighted and the representation of the composer was anatomically correct, Doc Widgett figured out, based on the size of Bach's head in comparison to the rest of him, that Bach had an I.Q. of 262. Now, 140 and up is considered to be genius and they get a Mensa application form, so either 262 is off-the-charts smart or the artist's eye was wonky.

However, when you look at Bach's music, the 262 seems to be dead on. Now, Colli always used to hate it when the ladies of the Central Committee of the Parsnip and Arts Fest would ask him who his FAVORITE composer was. He'd go into a tirade about superlatives, and "who's the best?" and "who's your fave?" and give them a lecture on looking at all composers for their unique contribution and appreciating all of them, NOT singling out with shamefully ignorant remarks like "Wagner's the best composer who ever lived!" (That one really got his dander up!)

But Colli did say, and would reiterate on more than one occasion, BACH WAS THE SMARTEST COMPOSER WHO EVER LIVED and he felt that way long before Doc Widgett's lecture at Squallor's Corners.

As well as being the SMARTEST composer who ever lived, there are two other important facts that are often overlooked in the plethora of verbiage that has been written about Bach over the 250 years since his death. And I'm going to bold-facedly state them right now and let them ricochet through your mental synapses and then we'll look at them in detail. (I always feel that there is much to be said in the learning process for shock value, so here goes!)

1. BACH NEVER WROTE ANY MUSIC FOR THE PIANO
2. BACH, like all great ones, IS TRANSFERABLE

Having recovered from the shock, let's look at them point by point.

1. Bach's dates are 1685-1750 – precisely the period when the pianoforte was being invented and developed. By the time of his death, it certainly hadn't reached the level of mechanical completion and perfection that it had by the 19th century. Bach had been raised on the harpsichord and was a master player himself as well as a church organist and so HE WROTE ALL OF HIS KEYBOARD MUSIC EITHER FOR THE ORGAN OR THE HARPSICHORD! NEVER FOR THE PIANO! And as you know by now, dear reader, a harpsichord is a very different instrument from a piano. The strings are plucked, not hammered, you can't grow louder or softer, there's no damper pedal to allow the strings to keep on vibrating, etc, etc. In a sense it's like Lucetta trying to fit into the Small size foundation garments from the Eaton's catalogue. The two don't fit. Harpsichord music played on a piano??? Impossible, you say!

No! and the reason is point number 2.

2. BACH IS TRANSFERABLE

When music is really great, when it goes beyond the scientific limitations of whatever instrument it's been written for and enters into that platonic ideal world of REAL MUSIC and not mere shadows of it, then it CAN BE TRANSFERRED to another medium and work equally well, if not better.

A case in point: Much of the Beatles' music has been transcribed and arranged for symphony orchestra and works a treat – a satisfying musical experience for both you rock and roll fans and us classicists. However, I've yet to hear a symphonic arrangement of *Great Balls of Fire* or *Rock Around the Clock*. It can be done, mind you, but as the original wasn't that great, so the transposition to another media is limited as well.

But not with BACH. Bach's keyboard works work brilliantly when played on the piano! Differently, but brilliantly. There are some pedantic purists who try to make their students play Bach on the piano and treat it as if it were a harpsichord. This is nuts! Utilize the full capabilities of the instrument to bring out all that's there in the music AND all that's implied in the music because it is capital-G Great music!

Before we go any further with old Bach, I think we need a brief list of his greatest keyboard music just so when we refer to "the 48" you're not going to be thinking of that Concession 48 road behind the creamery hill that goes down past the Hackler's Emu farm or the size-48 bra that Lucetta has to wear due to her amplitude.

A Brief List of Bach's Keyboard Works (not necessarily comprehensive):

The Well-Tempered Clavier, Bk. I
- 24 preludes & fugues in every major and minor key
The Well-Tempered Clavier, Bk. II
- ditto, he did it again

Together they are known as "The 48" and nobody else, no other composer, ever did 48 of the same thing and so you CAN say "thee 48" and everybody who knows will know what you are talking about and those who don't don't deserve to!

Two-part Inventions
Three-part Inventions
The Brandenberg Concerti (6)
Suites (English and French) and Partitas
Goldberg Variations
The Art of Fugue

Now, it is not the purvue of this tome to exhaustively evaluate or even describe in detail the keyboard works of Bach. You can find that in any old book about Bach.

My task is to encourage you to LISTEN to the works of what we really know as THEE FIRST GREAT KEYBOARD MASTER COMPOSER and beyond that just a few suggestions as to what to listen for.

What to Listen For When Listening to Bach:

A: Structure

Old man Bach was never frivolous and never wrote fluff. Plus, he composed in an era (Baroque) that was engrossed in form and organization and structure and even when his own sons were writing much more fluffy, frivolous stuff, daddy Bach stuck to the old tried and true ways he'd been used to and even got more complex as he got older. So listen with your MIND. Think about the music. Listen to what's going on. Don't be using it as background music for your fave movie of the week that you're watching in your imagination. LISTEN TO THE NOTES. No matter whether you have a PhD in music or you're a rank amateur lover of music without training, listen to the structure and form, to what's repeating or being developed, and you'll be happy as old Laetitia when she gets a good wallow in the mud in spring after a cold freeze-your-whatnots-off winter.

B: Musicality (Emotion and Feeling)

I can just hear some of you anal-retentive purists out there sayin' that this music is formal and structural, characteristic of the Baroque period and not your feely-feely agony-and-ecstasy Romantic gushes of the Romantic period. Now, while it *is* true that the music of this period and Bach's music specifically is structurally conceived and is concerned with pure Apollonian musical content, there is still, however, an EMOTIONAL SLASH SPIRITUAL level to Bach's works that combines heart and soul with the brain, producing a COMPLETE musical experience.

And just as Stravinsky stated that he was FREEST to compose when the RESTRICTIONS were the GREATEST, so it is possible, within the intellectual structured formality of Bach's works to pack in an intense amount of "musical" subtlety and emotional intensity.

Far too often, inferior pianists, challenged or overwhelmed by the technical complexities of Bach's works, start at the beginning and chomp through to the end and they may as well have typed it on Lucetta's old Olivetti Underwood. There wasn't an ounce of musicality in it at all. You must have complete mastery of the technical difficulties in any Bach work. You must have an intelligent understanding of what Bach has created formally and structurally and then, with ease and grace appropriate for the period (in his case, Baroque) find the "musicality" beneath, around, behind the notes themselves.

"If it ain't musical, it ain't worth playin' or hearin'" – and that is a direct quote from the Maestro himself!

Et Al.

If you notice in the table of contents and the title page, it refers to the Great One et al. While there have been a few Al's who were composers, that's not whom I'm talking about. It's Latin for "and others" and it's the other EARLY KEYBOARD COMPOSERS I want to discuss now.

Other Early Keyboard Composers:
Handel (George Frederick)
The German who bombed in Italy but then made it in England, primarily as an oratorio composer, as in the famous question-and-answer joke:
Q. Who wrote Handel's *Messiah*
A. Bach? ...or was it...???
Handel did write keyboard music and it's all right but it definitely is not as great as Bach's. Some of his suites aren't bad and, here and there, there's a delightful sarabande or courante, but not all great composers wrote great music all the time for all media. His *Messiah* was tops, so who cares if he was a bit artistically pooped in his keyboard works?
Scarlatti, Domenico
Described as the greatest harpsichordist who ever lived, he wrote over 550 sonatas for harpsichord, which are short two-movement pieces of unparalleled variety. They are brilliant little gems that really show off the tonal possibilities of the instrument. He spent most of his life working for the Queen of Spain and had actually been her teacher, and from my own experience, I can tell you it ain't easy working for most of the queens that I've worked for! They can be very demanding, God knows. When you read through a list of the characteristics of Scarlatti sonati, you realize that he certainly was more flamboyant than Bach and could betimes be a bit fluffy like most of Bach's sons. Here's a descriptive Scarlatti list:
lightning scales
hand-crossings
bone-crushing chords
infectious rhythms
melodic snatches

Do give him a listen. You all probably need a little lightning, crushing and crossing in your lives. It'll help you appreciate Bach all the more.

Chapter 7:
The even-more-famous S.O.B. and other Rococo-nuts

"Gird the loins of your mind," as Colli would say when he was about to launch into a significant discourse on a topic that had hitherto not received much attention, "We're in for a rough voyage, verbally speaking." And usually it was rough, particularly as the hours lengthened and the ales accumulated.

I, however, am in the bright sunlight by the sow pond (where Eustacia loves to lie) and I have only a jug of Lucetta's yarrow tea, a stimulating aphrodisiac whose primordial juices I'm hoping to thrust into this challenging chapter so that together, author and reader, we may come to the multiple delights of understanding that far supercede the original intentions of the aforementioned tea. So do, if you please, GIRD YOUR LOINS!

Bach (as in J.S. or old Bach) was reasonably famous in his day, although not so revered as he came to be later (and sadly – posthumously.)

He had tons of sons. Four of them were very well known. One, however, of the sons of Bach – or S.O.B.s, as they are sometimes called – was probably

THEE MOST FAMOUS S.O.B.

and certainly, for a book on the piano and its antecedents, a detailed discussion of him and his work is absolutely essential.

His name? Carl Philipp Emanuel Bach, hereafter CPE!

He performed on the clavichord, harpsichord, and even early versions of the pianoforte. He composed tons of works for clavier, orchestra, concerti & soli for instruments, oratorios, passions, and cantatas. He wrote a treatise called *Essays on the True Art of Playing Keyboard Instruments.*

He was also famous in his day, but then "history" took over and, as is so often the case, was cruel and neglectful. The 19th-century "Romantic" artists were so full of themselves that, apart from Felix Mendelssohn, they ignored Bach and all the S.O.B.s. Then in the 20th-century, history, people, et al., started to get excited about old man Bach (J.S.) but generally poo-pooed the sons as being "light" and "fluffy." Only recently, when the recording companies had recorded a gazillion versions of every 64th note old J.S. had ever written, did they have to start looking at the S.O.B.'s music, which is now more available mainly because they're running out of new old composers.

Lest you think that I – a lowly piano instructor in Chezlee Ont – am a lone voice in the wilderness crying out my praise for one S.O.B., may I quote some contemporaries – not mine but his – to bolster my case.

What people back then thought of CPE (the S.O.B.):

Mozart: "He is the father, we are the children. Those of us who do anything right, learned it from him. Whoever does not own to this is a scoundrel."

Muzio Clementi: "Whatever I know about fingering and the new style, in short, whatever I understand of the piano-forte, I have learned from this book [namely, CPE's essay]."

Dr. Charles Burney: "... he is not only one of the greatest composers that ever existed for keyboard instruments but the best player in point of expression."

Dr. Burney also put down CPE's dad when he said "... it would be difficult to trace ... how he [CPE] formed his style [which is] so different from the DRY AND LABOURED STYLE OF HIS FATHER!" (The capitals and the exclamation point are mine and not Burney's.)

Somebody else: "... to know Bach [CPE] completely one must hear:

a) the wealth of his imagination

b) the profound sentiment of his heart

c) his constant enthusiasm as he improvizes on his Silbermann clavichord

Haydn: Was also indebted to CPE but I couldn't find a quote. If you have one, send it in to me in care of Eebles Feed, Chezlee Ont and I'll include it in the 2nd edition and give you a free bag of Lucetta's rutabaga chips.

So you see, it's not just me but a veritable host of eminent persons who laud CPE. And now, I feel it is imperative that we look at what CPE had to say and let the S.O.B. speak for himself.

DIRECT QUOTES FROM THE S.O.B. HIMSELF

1. "My principal aim ... has been directed toward PLAYING AND COMPOSING AS VOCALLY AS POSSIBLE FOR THE KEY-BOARD DESPITE ITS DEFECTIVE SUSTAINING POWERS!" **

** I must interject strongly, urgently, and nay even excitedly with a "What ho? What ho? What do we have here???" Is this not a foretaste of what was to come more than 100 years later when Debussy would say (in French, of course) "Ya can't play a WHOLE NOTE on the piano!" CPE knew that! Already! Smack dab in the middle of the 18th century! Yet does he get the credit? Honestly now, I ask you! The number of times Colli and I have seen our ideas being "published" by others, our notes being "composed" by others … anyway, this is not the time or place and I still have to finish CPE's quote. To continue…

"…MUSIC MUST FIRST AND FOREMOST STIR THE HEART" **

** Anthon here, interjecting again, but I must. Things had gotten quite formally complex and intellectually overburdened toward the end of CPE's dad's life and era. The Baroque period used to end in 1750 (when his old man died), but realistically it ended in 1725, which was when the *Rococo* period started and lasted until 1775, when the Classical period began, and I think we need some adjectives here so we know where we're at – musically speaking:

ROCOCO
- decorative, elegant, hedonistic & frivolous
- the "gallant" style with emphasis on pleasantness and prettiness
- in Germany, although it meant "intimate expressiveness" it was however called EMPFINDSAMKEIT (just try to be light and fluffy and expressive when you try and say that!)

AND, while the French and Italians had a natural tendency to be a bit more "Rococo" then the Germans (particularly Old Man Bach), CPE, the S.O.B., was known as the outstanding master of Empfindsamkeit in the north of Germany, where things, and music especially, hadn't been light, fluffy or expressive for centuries, if ever! Hence, when CPE said music must STIR THE HEART, he was expressing the motto – the *crie de coeur* – of the Rococo period and all the Rococo-nuts who represented it. Now, to get on with the quote, which is actually only Number one!

"…THIS CANNOT BE ACHIEVED THROUGH MERE RATTLING, DRUMMING AND ARPEGGIATION." **

** Yet once again with the interjections, but it must be obvious. Did CPE himself attend the Wednesday evening

Women's Prayer and Crochet Fellowship at the First Baptist Church on 2nd Street and hear Thelma Tweeps play for the sing-song après prayer, before the sandwiches (no crust) and tea (milk only)? Because rattling, drumming and arpeggiation could not more accurately describe old Thelma. Now, as old as Thelma is, it must have been her ancestors that CPE heard and caused him to comment thusly.

In general, however, do you see how in this only the first direct quote of CPE himself I've had 3 (three) interjections already because of the extreme relevance to the musical scene today?

2.   DIRECT QUOTE #2 OF CPE the S.O.B.: "THE TRUE ART OF PLAYING KEYBOARD INSTRU-MENTS DEPENDS ON THREE FACTORS ...
CORRECT FINGERINGS
GOOD EMBELLISHMENTS ** AND
GOOD PERFORMANCE
But old CPE did establish in detail the importance of good fingering and good performance that HAS lasted to this day – among the superior teachers, of course. Not those upstarts at the New Chezlee Ont Conservatoire du Musique. Un peu de français is not going to cover up the fact that you, Selva Swagg, don't know a thing about piano playing. Anyways, everyone knows you're just in it for the money.

3. A LARGE DIRECT QUOTE from CPE the S.O.B (and I promise I won't interject):
"[there are] KEYBOARDISTS ... WHO AFTER TORTUR-OUS TROUBLE HAVE FINALLY LEARNED HOW TO MAKE THEIR INSTRUMENT SOUND LOATHSOME ... THEIR PLAY-ING LACKS ROUNDNESS, CLARITY, FORTH-RIGHTNESS, AND IN THEIR STEAD ONE HEARS ONLY HACKING, THUMPING AND STUMBLING. ALL OTHER INSTRUMENTS HAVE LEARNED HOW TO SING. THE KEYBOARD ALONE HAS BEEN LEFT BEHIND ..."

** In the 18th century, these were called ORNAMENTS and music was full of them. Little trills, mordents, turns and frou-frou – the chachka that was characteristic of the period but doesn't turn us on as much nowadays as it did then. Plus, or-naments changed from town to town, country to country, player to player, so who knows? And it's not worth getting your knick-ers in a knot about!

Again, old CPE reinforces the importance of "SINGING" at the keyboard. And here I hear the voice of my own piano instructor, who through a long and distinguished pedigree of teachers before her, taught the importance of SINGING the melody when playing the piano. Illusory as it is, non-sustaining as the keyboard is, it is nevertheless imperative that the PRETENSION of a SUNG-THROUGH-LINE be made, otherwise it ain't music.

There are simply too many quotes from this veritable cornucopia of keyboard teaching gems, so I can only encourage ANY serious student of the art of keyboard playing to get a copy and read it. However, I will give you a point-form paraphrased list of bonbons, which will stimulate you no end. I hope.

(MORE) STIMULATING BONBONS FROM CPE (para phrased):

- Full harmonies, requiring three or more instruments can be expressed by a keyboard ALONE! Yeah!
- Those who've achieved renown, musically, usually are excellent keyboardists.
- Since I published my *Essay* ... teaching and playing have improved.
- Since I published my *Essay*, tons of textbooks have been written plagiarizing me left, right and centre, but what pees me off the most is that they make mistakes when they steal or steal out of context. I can assert without anger and in truth that every instruction book that I have seen since the publication of my essay is FILLED WITH ERRORS. And I can prove it, so there!

I must stop, dear friends, but as you see I could go on and on. Each page is yet another rich mine field of diamonds and sapphires and educational emeralds that make you humbly aware that not everything has been discovered only in one's lifetime. But even in those times of CPE, without TV or plumbing or rocket science or planes or electric razors or microwaves, they did know something about playing the piano. If I may, I'll end the CPE S.O.B. section with one last quote, which I think is so wise in this age of "Learn to play the piano and the *Moonlight Sonata* in 10 weeks at the 88 Keys School for Playing, for only $795.00 Cdn (cash only)."

CPE's quote: "Nothing fundamental can be learned with out time and patience."
Were there other ROCOCO-NUTS like CPE? Yes and No! There were a few good ones, like:
François COUPERIN
Georg TELEMANN
Johann MATTHESON
Domenico SCARLATTI
Johann STAMITZ
and there are ROCOCO elements in Mozart and Haydn.
BUT
Things also went kind of downhill as well in this period, which is a risk you take if the period's aim is to be pretty, frivolous, lighthearted and gay. We all know the trouble that can get you into. Anyway here's a list of ROCOCO-NUTS that you'll probably never ever hear of again. They come under this title:
DETERIORATION OF ARTISTIC STANDARDS OCCURRED UNDER MUSICIANS SUCH AS:
Balbastre
Daquin
Nichelmann
Graziolo
Sacchini
and many others.
These obviously were among the thumpers and the wackers, the plagiarizers and misquoters that CPE mentions so frequently in his *Essay*. And, may I say, when he goes on his critical bent, he does, he does, he does remind me of our DEAR MAESTRO COLLI ALBANI, who does go on a negative bent quite frequently, and remembering these bents has tearfully reminded me of his absence, so I'm off to the Ox & Udder to have a nostalgic nip in fond remembrance. Also, I have to get a new pen, 'cause this one's run out on this somewhat verbose chapter.
P.S. Seven years after CPE died, Haydn dropped in to Hamburg on his way home to Vienna from London, hoping to see him for a visit. Needless to say, he was disappointed. He obviously had not read the obits.

Chapter 8:
CLASSICUS MAXIMUS –
Three Biggies and ½ of Beethoven

It is days since I finished the last chapter. I have been pacing in the asparagus patch, whittling in the woods and in general procrastinating the daunting task of trying to tackle the music of the three biggies of the Classical Period (Haydn, Mozart and Schubert (sort of)) and the first half of Beethoven.

I do miss Colli. I need that inspiration, that kick he was always able to give me in my intellectual arse that would spur me on. It is hard providing one's own spurs and indeed I had despaired of ever commencing the chapter until last Sunday, in the middle of the Rev. McDudd's sermon on "the Book of Revelation and certain flooding occurring south of Bognor's Swamp," I thought, "If that idiot can stand up in front of the pulpit and preach as nonsensical a sermon as this, surely I can do the same on the subject of the Classical Masters." And so I shall.

There is so much already written about the Viennese Classical greats that I must limit my remarks to their music for the piano and certain perhaps not-so-well-known anecdotes about their lives that would help to elucidate their raison d'être as well as their magnum opuses-es.

We start with Franz Joseph Haydn and look first at his personal anecdotes.

Haydn's personal anec-dotes that may (or not) effect his music:

HAYDN'S WIFE USING HIS MANUSCRIPTS FOR HAIR CURLERS.

1. His wife would shred his manuscripts to make curlers for her hair. As well as a shredder, she was also a shrew-er and that's why perhaps Haydn was content to work out in the country at Prince Esterházy's estate, away from home.

2. He obviously didn't need papers or keep up to date on who died because, as we learned in the last chapter, it wasn't very fruitful visiting Carl Philip Emanuel Bach seven years after he died.

3. He was the second of 12 children and poor.

4. He was so poor he lived in an attic, practised the clavier and violin and became a servant to the opera composer Porpora, for which he got free composition lessons. God knows what he had to do for Porpora to get free lessons.

5. Eventually he became famous, rich and even happy – mostly because he got seperated from that bitch of a wife who used his sonatinas for hair curlers (see opposite).

6. For two years 1792-4, he tried to teach Beethoven but "it was difficult ..."

7. King George III (who was nuts anyway – did you see the movie???) gave Haydn a talking parrot to take home when he declined George's invitation to spend the summer of '95 at Windsor Castle. Castle or no, Haydn didn't want to be cooped up with a nutbar for the summer and wisely preferred the company of a mimicing bird that merely said "Pretty Polly" when you said "Pretty Polly" to it. Come to think of it, that was about what George was capable of.

Speaking of the movie, do you know when they brought it to the United States, they couldn't call it *The Madness of George III* because the Americans would have thought that, like *Rocky I* through *VIII*, they would have missed the first two movies in the series and therefore wouldn't go to see George III? I guess it's a cultural difference, but my stars ...!

Haydn's Music for the Piano:

1. He wrote more than 50 sonatas for the piano but they're not that hot! His other stuff was much better. This is clear even today, as great pianists are known as a Mozart specialist, a Bach specialist, a Beethoven specialist. But who has ever heard of a Haydn specialist? Eh?

2. None of his piano sonatas was written in New Jersey, U.S.A.

This misunderstanding comes from the Dutch musicologist Anthon Van Hoboken, whose numbering system for the sonatas is in general use – eg. *Sonata in D*, Hob. 19.

Haydn did travel a lot in his life, but he never visited the home town of Frank Sinatra in New Jersey cause it hadn't been built yet.

3. The three "best ones" i.e. Hob. 50-52, were written for a Mrs. Bartolozzi, a pianist who lived in London and hence the first one is called the *English Sonata*. I think it's interesting that the only decent piano sonatas were written for a lady friend. Did Mrs. Bartolozzi (they were all called Mrs. in those times) provide Haydn with some of the joy his slovenly "ex" had never given him? Was there a renewed spark in his life that finally pushed his piano sonatas into something worthwhile and on par with the fine quartets and great symphonies and all the other wonderful music Haydn wrote? Why was it that his piano music was at the bottom of excellence in his magnificent pile of work? Did the legs of his spinet remind him of the ex- Mrs. Haydn's legs? Did she play his piano works herself and so subtlely he didn't want her to play beautifully because she used his sonatinas for hair curlers and it was a twisted form of revenge? These are all questions inquiring minds want to know and, as yet, are unanswered.

MOZART

There is absolutely no point in discussing virtually any of the anecdotal detail of this great genius's life as you've either read them all in books, bought the video of the movie or seen the play, so there's very little this rural instructor can add.

The only points that perhaps are worth reiterating are a remark once made in a letter to his sister in which he confessed that "pissing" gave him more pleasure than composing and the fact that his masterpieces "came" to him complete and finished and unedited and would proceed from his brain through his pen to the manuscript paper. And there it would be launched to the world, perfect in every respect.

Regarding Mozart's music for keyboard:

1. It's important to remember that he was a concert pianist from the age of 6, when he first performed for the emperor. He knew the keyboard intimately and professionally from a very early age, so when he wrote piano music, he knew what he was doing.

2. Mozart means exactly what he writes. You follow exactly what the score indicates, adding only the appropriate understanding of the nature of the music of his time and that indefinable "musicality" and you end up being a Mozart specialist.

3. If you've mastered the basic technique of piano playing over six to eight years and you're looking for a starting-off point in the truly great piano music, then Mozart is a good place to start. Each piece a gem of simplistic challenges and complex accessability that will delight the student at every level of learning.

4. Playing Mozart is like living in a glass house. Everything is visible. Nothing can be hidden. Unlike Beethoven or the Romantics, where wetter (that's heavier) pedalling can attempt to hide the odd musical indiscretion, everything shows in Mozart. The slightest sin is heard with resounding clarity. An overly stressed note in an accompanying figure can stick out like the crudest wart on a witch's nose. The student must not be discouraged by these standards of absolute perfection, but rather consider them a challenge to be met patiently yet with determination.

5. His sonatas, concerti, variations, etc. represent, after the 48 et al. of Bach, the next great contribution to the literature for the piano.

6. Remember the pianoforte he wrote for was in the process of becoming what it is today – but like Bach, all music of greatness is capable of perfect transposition to the Steinways and Bösendorfers of today.

7. How sad that poverty, overwork and illness finished him off at the tender age of 35. And yet, the legacy he left ...!

SCHUBERT

Now, when it comes to Schubert, there are a lot of questions raised one way or another about a lot things, so we will deal with them thusly:

Questions concerning Schubert:

1. Why was he a bit overweight and had to wear glasses?
2. Why did he never leave Vienna in his entire life?
3. Was it really typhoid fever that killed him at age 31? If not, what was it?

4. Why was he so impoverished? Did he enjoy it?

5. a) Was he too close to his mother and what was the exact nature of his relationship with his small intimate coterie of male friends?

b) There's a lot of enigmatic "pain" talked about in his letters: What's that all about?

6. While he idealized Beethoven, why did he prefer the gentler, lighter tones of Mozart, Haydn, and Clementi?

7. Why did he call the playing style of the distinguished concert pianists of his day "accursed banging which can please neither the ear nor the senses?"

8. Why did he never write a piano concerto?

9. He seems awfully "Romantic" for a classical composer. How come?

10. Do his 20 sonatas, impromptus, *moments musicaux*, dances and over 600 accompaniments to his songs constitute a body of piano literature on a par with Bach and Mozart? If not, why not?

11. If he was so unhappy, why are his *Marches Militaires* referred to as "gay?"

12. In describing his works, e.g. *Bb-major Piano Sonata* D. 960, who was "D"? And what was his relationship with him?

13. If he's not in your top 10, why not? He should be!

The answers to these and other questions about Schubert are cryptically listed in subsequent pages of this book based on anagrams of four of the astrological signs. The answers are also patently self-evident to the simplest of students with heads on their shoulders.

What I'd encourage you to do is form a Schubertiade discussion group at your home. Invite friends and serve tea and sorbet and start finding answers to these and other questions about Schubert and other questionable composers.

THE FIRST ½ OF BEETHOVEN

Beethoven was one of those great figures known as a TRANSITIONAL figure, who spans two distinct periods and styles and is the primary agent that takes us from one to the other.

The other kind of great figure is known as a SUM-MER UPPER. They come at the end of an era and pull it all together in a great summation of their particular period.

There are also some who just start and keep going to the end and I like to call them your basic PLODDING GENIUSES, of which, modestly I think the Maestro and I are among, although with more emphasis on the plodding and not quite so much on the genius.

Here is a small comparison chart to give you an idea of what I'm talking about:

GREAT TRANSITIONAL GUYS
MONTEVERDI
from Renaissance to Baroque
BEETHOVEN
from Classical to Romantic
GREAT SUM – MER UPPERS
PALESTRINA
the Renaissance
BACH
the Baroque
MOZART
the Classical
PLODDING GENIUS'S
MAESTROCOLLI ALBANI, L.C.B.O.
More of a genius ME (Prof. ANTHON
E. DARLING, B.S.)
More of a plodder.

And since Beethoven was transitional between two periods, he has to be dealt with between two chapters. In the next chapter we'll deal with his Romantic half. For the present we'll look at his Classical half.

Now, before we even look at the first ½ of Beethoven, there's another category in which we need to discuss him and that is this:

THERE ARE TWO (2) TYPES OF GENIUSES:
A. INSPIRED FROM THE TOP DOWN, VIRTUALLY EFFORTLESSLY
And
B: WORKED OUT FROM THE BOTTOM UP, WITH BLOOD, SWEAT AND TEARS

Now most of us, and I include myself humbly in that pile, fall somewhere in the middle, whereby occasionally we get inspired to do something but for the most part it's workin' it out with a lot of sweat and tears. I've never drawn blood from composing. Just the asparagus shredder when I got too close to it last fall.

However, let me show you two of the best examples of these categories:

A: *Mozart*

- he heard the entire symphony in his head all the way through, beginning to end, before he wrote out a single note. And when he started to write, he'd write out the first flute all the way through, then the second flute ....

- his scores therefore were neat as a pin and never messy and scratched out with corrections. He simply wrote out what he'd heard in his head

- as indicated earlier in this very chapter, taking a leak gave him more pleasure than composing, so that indicates the below-bodily-function regard with which he held his composing genius

- his music tends to be perfect and complete. When stuff comes "down from above" it tends to be perfect, whereas the other B-category stuff sometimes could do with some fixing up.

- Mendelssohn was also this kind of genius: He could go to a concert, hear a symphony for the first and only time, then come home and write the entire symphony out note by note beginning to end. Now, that's some genius. I've heard Colli, at a special Arts Fest Annual Meeting when he's gotten into a bit too much of the Parsnip merlot, start *O Canada* and end up with the Star Spankled Planner, but that's another influence.

-The Mozartian and Mendelssohnian type of geniuses, tend to function as a kind of CONDUIT, a MEDIUM, a VESSEL whereby the extra-terrestrial is brought to Earth. They're a kind of maitre d' for the universe, standing at the mortal portals, saying, "And may I present a little piece from the Jupiter galaxy ... "

B: *Beethoven*

- one of the messiest composers of all time. His scores are full of scratches, crossouts, x's, lunch and breakfast and what have you. His genius is definitely the working-it-out-from-the-bottom-up-with-blood-sweat-and-tears-and-old-fried-egg type of genius.

- you can hear the struggle and effort in the music itself as it tries to lift itself out of the basement of art into the attic of great masterpieces

- that's why so many people like his music, however, because they identify with the struggle that's there in every bar

- as a result, the music he wrote at the end of his life was diametrically different from the music he wrote near the beginning. It's a long way from the basement to the attic and the views are quite different.

- strangely enough, neither Beethoven (nor myself) ever married and I think those of us that work it out from the bottom up just don't have the time. We're always struggling, improving, searching, and longing, which doesn't leave us a lot of time for dating or pursuing. Whereas the inspired genius is so more relaxed that between getting "zapped" by a symphony, then a wind octet, he can enjoy a bit of rumpy-pumpy or play a bit of fox in the hen house 'cause his genius mind has been "flushed" waiting for a "refill." Us bottom-to-uppers are constantly fussing and fuming about how to find a theme for our next first movement or what to do with it when we've found it. This leaves you in a constantly vulnerable, yet challenging state, which I must confess – and I speak here for myself entirely and not Beethoven – I do enjoy.

Having defined Beethoven as a TRANSITIONAL FIGURE who nevertheless WORKED IT OUT FROM THE BOTTOM UP WITH BLOOD, SWEAT AND TEARS, there are still a few additional points we need to look at before we can discuss either half of him. And per usual we'll use the helpful point form:

Point 1: Not everything Beethoven wrote was clean spanking perfect and reeking of genius.

Let me qualify this bold statement while you're recovering from the massive implications and say that if it wasn't sheer genius, it was pretty damn good, just not AS great.

This is a typical dilemma for those of us in the WORK IT OUT category. Sometimes we just aren't able to work it out. Sometimes the publishing deadline arrives and we have to dry the ink and send it off, saying, "I wish I could have done better but the rent is due at the end of the month and the coal bill has to be paid, so for this little Bagatelle Opus Who? Number What? that's as good as it's gonna get, and if they don't like it, they can shove that little Bagatelle wherever they like."

Do you see what I mean? And this is more characteristic of Beethoven – the first half – when he was working within the confining chains of Classicism. When he finally "broke out" into Romanticism, things got better. Sometimes they got pretty wild and way out but they were never "mediocre" – the worst thing you can say about a creative genius. *

* I know, 'cause it's been said of me so often. Please understand, I am not belittling his suffering. For a musician/composer to lose his or her hearing is the cruelest twist of fate. However, by that very ironic twist, his suffering became the model, the pattern, the mold by which subsequent artists would try to fashion themselves. And putting the cart before the horse, they tried to suffer so much so that they could possibly be considered as a genius.

The thought that one could be a happily married, financially well-off, normal, respected musician or composer or artist became INCOMPREHENSIBLE to the Romantic notions of the 19th century and dribbled on into the 20th century and indeed into my own back yard and upbringing.

I constantly felt that if I didn't win first prize in the Chezlee and Environs Country Piano Festival, it was not because I hadn't practised enough. NO! It was because I hadn't SUFFERED enough.

"Look at Beethoven," I was told. How often in my teenage years I tried to "go deaf" just so I could become a great composer. But to no avail. Now I'm not saying that Beethoven did this. It was his successors, his followers, his disciples, if you will, who took his life and nailed it on the cross of GREAT ART and made his suffering the standard, the norm by which great artists were to be judged. While his genius is unquestionable and his greatness universally accepted, his posthumous shadow loomed larger than the man himself and created worshippers far more fanatical than the one they revered.

Now, I don't know about you, but my brain hurts and I think we'll learn just as much about Beethoven's first half when we look at his transition into his second half in the next chapter, so I'm going to leave matters right here and have a Stoney Ripple.

Have one yourself, for Pete's sake, and pick up tomorrow where you left off tonight, why dontcha?

Point 2: Beethoven was messy.

Here again is where I feel a great sense of personal identification with the man.

His scores were a mess

His hair was a mess

His apartments were a mess

His clothes were a mess!

There was very little about him that wasn't messy. Now, usually these types tend to hook up with Miss Neat Freak – the spic & span duster-upper of the universe who loves a challenge and strangely wants to marry it. Well, she either never came along or Beethoven was just too messy for anyone to live with in a relationship. And I must say I'm grateful to both Lucetta and the Maestro for putting up with my not-quite-so-neat-ness, although I must say that both of them are not that far away themselves from the living standards of our sows. But we muddle around together in rural bliss, whereas Beethoven was always getting heck from his landladies for peeing in a bucket and not bathing for weeks on end.

Point 3: Beethoven suffered and furthermore became the MODEL FOR SUFFERING for most of the artists of the 19th century and most of the wannabe artists of the 20th century.

An Ode: Students I've Loved (or NOT!)

When it comes to a recollection of the plethora of students, young and old, that have stumbled up the cow-dung-strewn path to the "front" room of Obscuria and have sat down at our ancient grand, to be instructed in the art of pianoforte playing, my mind revels and rambles, rejoices and repugnates. Mostly, however, they are pleasant memories that are impossible to sum up in any kind of categorized compendium. And so, in my usual fashion, I shall amble down the avenue of a few specifics and from these you will be able to draw your own conclusions as to the whole.

I shall discuss them in the following numerical order that is in no way indicative of their worth or my feelings about them or their progress:

1. The McGilliguddy boy
2. Miss Myrtle Whimsby
3. Doris Scraggs
4. That little Fludd boy
5. Gretchen Ringwald – a foreign-exchange student from down Highway 6

THE M^cGILLIGUDDY BOY   MISS MYRTLE WHIMSBY   DORIS SCRAGGS   THAT LITTLE FUDD BOY   GRETCHEN RINGWALD FROM DOWN

The McGilliguddy Boy

Probably one of the most talented pupils I've ever had the privilege of teaching. His ability to play was virtually natural and intrinsic. I had little to do but suggest here, encourage there, and out would come such wonderful sounds that I felt he was possibly on his way to a concert career. Betimes I would bemuse myself, during a slow Brahms or a reflective adagio of

Hummel or Spohr, by picturing the young McGilliguddy boy at a Steinway or Bösendorfer in Carnegie Hall and myself nervously hiding in the wings waiting to hear his ultimate cadenza and anticipating the thunderous ovation that would ensue upon his final cadence.

His parents were simple but arduous folk who had gotten into Black Angus Beef semen production and cornered not only the local market but had made inroads into the national and international markets. Their semen was vying on the world's top bovine stages and winning and the McGilliguddy fortunes were growing. They generously put the money into the artistic education of their only boy so he wouldn't have to look at what they'd looked at for years in order to get rich (see above under bull semen for what they'd looked at).

At 16, I knew we were reaching that critical time when the McGilliguddy boy had to make a decision about a concert career. It was the first time in my entire teaching life that I had been placed in that position and I was delirious with anticipated excitement.

Having outlined the challenges of a concert career, the hardships, the pain, the loneliness, but also the ultimate adulation and fame and the rewards of a lifetime devoted to the delectable delights that music offers, I eagerly awaited his response with bated breath *and* tenterhooks.

To quote the McGilliguddy boy exactly would probably give you the best picture and reason as to why I ended up at the Ox & Udder that night, Stoney Rippled out of my mind.

"Are you kidding?" said the McGilliguddy boy, "Why would I want to be poor like you? I want to be rich like my parents. No way, José!" I was stunned. The boy's logic had worked thusly:

Mom and Dad, by means of Bull Semen, become RICH

Prof. Anthon E. Darling, by means of Music, remains POOR.

My splutterings about the "joy of music" the "rich rewards of aesthetic appreciation" and the $1.95 an hour he could get teaching little brats to play *The Flowers that Bloom in the Spring, Tra-La* fell squarely on deaf ears.

The McGilliguddy boy stopped lessons shortly after that and immediately upon graduation went into bull semen so seriously that the family business quadrupled. He writes me a postcard occasionally from his yacht/condo in whatever port

he happens to be harboring and the content is usually the same:
"Yo, Darling!
How's it hanging?
Still doin' that music thing?
I'll fly up in my jet to see ya
sometime in old Chez-lee, eh?
Hang loose"

                                        The McGilliguddy Boy

There's never a return address, so I never reply. I simply
pause a moment, reflect on the last time he played the Debussy
Arabesque 2ieme and have myself a little cry.

Miss Myrtle Whimsby

Miss Whimsby had worked most all of her life for the Electric Company as a bookkeeper. And somewhere in "mid-life" decided to add the pursuit of piano playing to her other passions,
which were cross-stitching and African violets.

Myrtle played "by the book" and took ever so long to get any
degree of pianistic proficiency. But to her credit she did make it.
Her renditions, however, were square and proper and lacked,
particularly the Romantic compositions, the fire and passion
that were required to play them properly.

How to put the fire and passion into Miss Whimsby's noc-
turnes and impromptus became my pedagogical goal. How could
I speak of love requited or unrequited to a Presbyterian cross-
stitcher who was a life member of the Chezlee Ont Temper-
ance Women's Auxiliary and the Baptist Ladies Prayer Guild
and Baby Sets Knitting Group? There was one Schubert impromptu in particular that Myrtle would "execute" without the
slightest ounce of feeling. I simply could not remain awake for
the entire piece, as she bored it to death.

I would play it for her myself, pouring my very soul into
every bar, using the principal of "effective memory recall," I
brought up all the turgid moments, the rhapsodic ecstasies, the
agonies, and the raptures of my personal past, and infused every
16th note of that Schubert with every emotional fibre of my being.

Exhausted, spent and perspiring, I turned to Myrtle and
said,
"There!"
"That was lovely" monotoned Myrtle.

"Would you play it please? Again? Just like that?" I pleaded "Surely, Professor Darling" she murmured.

And she sat down at the piano and rendered THEE AB-SOLUTELY UTTERLY MOST DEADLY DULL BORING VER-SION OF THE IMPROMPTU I HAD EVER HEARD IN MY LIFE.

When it was finally over, like some extended jail sentence, I sighed, "What can I say?... What CAN I say??? ..."

She cancelled her lesson the following week due to a "cold," the next week due to "coming down with something," the follow-ing two weeks due to relatives visiting from the States and on and on until it had been three months since she'd been for a lesson. I was beginning to worry, until ...

It was a hot August evening when she next arranged to come for a lesson. As soon as she entered the house, I knew some-thing was different. The hair, formerly neat as a pin, was slightly disheveled but in that French way – a cautious careful planned casualness that is subtly evocative. The traditional blouse had been replaced by a looser fitting flowing silk top that was NOT buttoned to the very top. It was not undone to the floozy-point but again, open enough for a demure tease. Solid, sensible shoes had been replaced by higher, thinner heels and an aubergine suede skirt that sparkled, reflecting the pi-ano light.

The normal formalities having been dispensed with, I casu-ally queried, "What would you like to play first?" still stunned by the incredible change, though delicate and tasteful, that had oc-curred in Miss Whimsby. Little did I know that the visual changes were minuscule in comparison with the aural shocks I was about to receive.

"Here goes!" says Myrtle, in a cheerier way than I'd ever heard her speak. She then followed it with a totally uncharacter-istic, "Fasten your safety belt, Anthon!"

Anthon. Anthon! She'd never called me Anthon in 13 years of lessons with me. What's happened?

From the first bar I knew the answer. The first phrase was delicately phrased, coming almost to the peak then holding, then teasing, then spilling out through the climax into the clos-ing notes of the phrase. And we were only in bar 3. Bar after bar surged on, phrase after phrase piled on top of each other, each one shaped and molded with the delicate artistry of a master craftsman infusing the music with intense feeling and passion and playing the keys like a luring temptress seduces her prey. I could not believe my ears. I was her helpless victim as she played with my musical heartstrings, taunted my ears and tantalized my senses, using Schubert as her aphrodisiacal enticement.

When her hands finally lifted from the keys after an over-extended lingering onto the last notes like a post-coital *Craven A*, she turned to me, almost coquettishly and smiled, "There, is that better?" and laughed lowly.

My natural shyness and modesty prevented me from expressing the thoughts that were pouring through my mind in that moment. – I did NOT say

1.   You've had sex
2.   You've had sex with a man
3.   You've enjoyed having sex with that man
4.   Was it just one man?
5.   Or was it a woman?

No, I said none of these things and only murmured awkwardly things like "Wow!" and "What a difference!" and "Boy, oh boy" and "Gosh, I can hardly wait to hear your *Pathétique* second movement."

She played it then and it was better than the Schubert: controlled, mature but expression-packed. The lessons became more sporadic but they were infinitely more enjoyable. No wedding bells ever rang for Miss Whimsby and I never found out who it was that had unleashed her Schubert et al. – although I did have my suspicions, but they were never substantiated.

Doris Scraggs

Doris Scraggs was unfortunately one of those people who always end up being referred to as "poor" and poor Doris had many reasons for being adjective-ified thusly. Poor Doris had had some rough disappointments in her background and the circumstances of life had not been easy on her. The result of this negative accumulation was that Doris was in PERMANENT THERAPY. Every task was undertaken in an effort to see "if it would help." Nothing was ever done for its own sake. It was all to assuage her pain, her tortured whatever.

Now, while, as a piano teacher, I have always performed the role of a kind of armchair psychiatrist for the little bumps that come a-cropping in the lives of my students, I have never felt qualified to take on the bigger problems that some folk have. Doris was already seeing a shrink twice a week, so I settled down to focus on music as a tool to assist in her general therapy and nothing else.

One lesson, as she was laboring through a fairly pedestrian Kuhlau sonatina, the tears started to roll down her cheeks and sniffling and sighing turned to deep sobbing.

Now, Kuhlau was a pre-Romantic composer and there really is rarely, if ever, anything in his music that would give rise to a reaction of this calibre. Doris was obviously dealing (or not) with something way beyond Kuhlau.

It was impossible for me to know what to do as the sobbing increased and the tempo of the Kuhlau decreased to a funeral dirge.

Suddenly, with a ginormous sob, Doris cried "I must dance! Play!" and with that she stood up from the rickety piano stool and began to gyrate and gesticulate about the room in a semi-aesthetic fashion. I slid onto the stool and, following orders, began to play, praying to St. Cecilia, the patron saint of the musical arts, to guide my fingers over the keys to play what ever was needed in the situation to help poor Doris.

Well, you know, for the next 35 minutes, I improvised and Doris did expressive dancing, sort of in the line of Isadora Duncan with intermittent sobbing, groaning and sometimes ripples of gentle laughter. At the end of the allotted time for for the "piano lesson," she quite matter-of-factly stopped, paid her $1.95 as usual for the lesson, dried her tear-stained face with a tissue and said, "Thank you, that was quite helpful! Next week same time? And I may need to dance again. OK?"

"Sure" I said, still with a stunned feeling that I had been watching something happen to me over which I had had absolutely no control but that had been, in retrospect, not an unpleasant experience. St. Cecilia or some spirit from some world beyond my conscious mind had indeed guided my fingers over the 88 and I wished I had taped the "session" and had a permanent record of the music that had transpired.

Poor Doris continued to come and Kuhlau and Schmitt were never touched again. St. Cecilia conducted the lesson and Doris sobbed and sighed and felt much better. She upped the number of lessons to two per week and when finances were forcing her to cut down again to just once a week, old Doc Chambers, the Chezlee shrink, said, "Cut down on one of your visits to me, but keep seeing Prof. Darling twice a week. Whatever he's doing in Obscuria is helping you a damn site more than I am."

I report this not in any way to boast, for I do give the credit to St. Cecilia, but simply to relate one of the strangest and yet most heavenly experiences of my entire teaching career.

Doris eventually eased up on the number of lessons and finally stopped and I heard latterly that she left town, married, and opened a small café in Clapperton called the Tarte and Pekoe and was relatively happy.

That Little Fludd Boy

That Little Fludd boy was an unholy terror. The first years were spent trying to get him to SIT on the stool for the majority of the lesson. The next level was to try to get him to play a piece from beginning to end without stopping. Any devious means to avoid whatever it was I was trying to teach would be employed. The worst stunt he ever pulled was the time he was about age 11. The lesson-slash-torture time was finally over and I muttered a relieved-slash-terrified, "I'll see you next week ..." and watched him exit by the somewhat dilapidated front screen door.

Exhausted, depleted and discouraged, I schlepped to the kitchen to make a cup of tea to restore my sagging spirits. I can't remember what else I did in the following 22 minutes until I ended up sitting in my favorite tub chair, lost in some musicological thought and enjoying the soothing massage of silence.

At exactly 23 minutes AFTER that little Fludd boy had left, he SUDDENLY JUMPED UP FROM BEHIND THE TUB CHAIR AND YELLED "BOO!" The shock was SO GREAT, my leap from the chair was more a levitation than a jump. My head hit the ceiling. I clutched at my heart, certain that cardiac arrest was imminent. Between my yelling and screaming and that little Fludd boy's yelps of delight that his scheme had succeeded, the noise rose to such a din that the hens in the chicken house went into a laying frenzy, three of the sows ran to the slough and wallowed and Lucetta came running up from the asparagus patch ready to call the police.

I had never ever received such a shock in my life. That little Fludd boy had cleverly snuck back in, after my back was turned, and waited silently in the semi-darkness of dusk in absolute total silence for that extremely lengthy period of time until he knew – AND HE DID KNOW – the precise moment that would achieve the maximum shock.

Somewhere, in that pre-adolescent volcano of his mind, he must have realized that he had come close to committing teacher-cide and after that, the guilt must have actually driven him to learn how to play the piano. However, with full-blown puberty he found far more enjoyable things to play with than Clementi sonatinas and he quit.

He phoned me once to tell me he was about to become quite rich from an invention he'd made. It was a device to hold up the toilet seat when men are relieving themselves in the standup position. He said he'd always been frustrated by the fact that men had to have one hand on the toilet seat to keep it up, and the other hand guiding the specific functioning body member in the ablutionary exercize. I thought that this was a lovely helpful idea and perhaps he was in some small way trying to atone for his earlier pranks against humanity and me specifically.

His invention obviously did not take off and earn him gazillions of moolah, as I still find myself in the DOUBLE-HOLD position in the lavatory. I did hear, however, that latterly he had, for some unknown reason, joined the French Foreign Legion and served in North Africa for two years and had then been released from his duties (*sans honneur!*) Why the French Foreign Legion would have hired that little Fludd boy in the first place has always remained a mystery to me. Or was it some kind of sentence he had received for misdemeanors far in excess of scarring the daylights out of a lonely piano instructor in Chezlee Ont?

Gretchen Ringwald

I was going to write about Gretchen Ringwald, my foreign-exchange student from Billiousville, down Highway 6, but her relatives still maintain influence at a high level in county affairs and the bitterness still remains and permeates to this day after what happened. So not wishing to reopen old wounds,

I shall not go into the GRETCHEN recollection, except to say that the whole incident was in no way initiated, or even hinted at, by yours truly and if she'd been focusing on what I was trying to teach her about Schmitt and the structure of a fugue, we would never have gotten involved in the mess we did. I have no faith whatsoever in the local judiciary system, particularly since it's her uncle who is the county circuit judge and who is HE going to believe, even if he is sober enough to hear what's going on in court?

It just goes to show you the dangers involved in fugal analysis when the subject starts on the dominant and the answer comes in on the tonic. The garden path to Hell which that discussion led us to is not to be believed and the fact that she locked herself in our indoor W.C. with those pills is such a mean form of emotional blackmail. What was I to do? Honestly, I ask you.

Anyway, the whole beastly affair is now long gone and forgotten and apart from that one brief and nasty appearance at the divorce trial, I and Obscuria have come out relatively unscathed. The rumor mill I cannot be responsible for and God knows the Chezlee Ont version of the rumor mill produces some of the most fanciful and malicious strains of gossip produced anywhere in the world.

So it's best just to let the whole thing go and get on with things. I know I have, so that's why I'm not saying anything at all about it, especially in print, where excerpts can be quoted and people can string you up on a lynchpost for what you've said. That's why I'm remaining completely close-mouthed about the whole thing and, as a matter of fact, I'm going to end this whole chapter right now, 'cause it's left a certain bitter taste in my mouth that only a good toast at the Ox & Udder can rectify, so I'm off. See you in the next chapter, whatever that is.

Chapter 9:
Busted Wires and Broken Movements –
the Other ½ of Beethoven

In the history of music (and agriculture) there are, from time to time, great geniuses that come along and STRADDLE two very different styles or periods and, frequently, are the major cause of that change. One of the titles used to describe these straddling genii is TRANSITIONAL FIGURE. You have already learned that the great STRADDLER, the TRANSITIONAL FIGURE we're talking about, is the German composer Ludwig van Beethoven, since we only discussed Beethoven – the first half – earlier in the chapter before last. And as he obviously had a 'later or 'second' half, I'm sure the question arose, "How did his later differ from his early?" And to help you understand I have an example:

In Chezlee Ont we always mark the spring of '76 as a watershed – an historical turning point – in the development of our agrarian burg, for '76 was the year that Belva and Barfley Birtwhistle changed their annual crop from barley to beets and the repercussions that event had on our little bucolic hamlet have been earth-shattering. Not the least of which, beyond the economic and agricultural consequences, was the sudden breakup of Belva and Barfley's 20-year nuptial relationship – and all "Cuz o' the beets!" (to quote Belva herself).

Before '76, we were known as a "barley" community, after '76, we were known as a beet community, for just about everybody else switched from grains to beets because they wanted to be "with the times"!

The amazing coincidence, and the very reason I used this particular local analogy, is that Ludwig van Beethoven's very name, when translated from the German becomes –

LOUIS OF THE BEET FIELDS !!!!!!

The intricate interconnections and cosmic significance of musicological scholarship, at times, are overwhelming. And this last one has done it to me so I'm going to have a Stoney Ripple just to bring my blood pressure down ....

There.... That's better, and before going into a pile of repetitive verbiage about my analogy, why don't I simply give you a diagramatic drawing, which says it all so much better:

Do you see it?
Do you see the great STRADDLER?
The TRANSITIONAL FIGURE that Beethoven was?

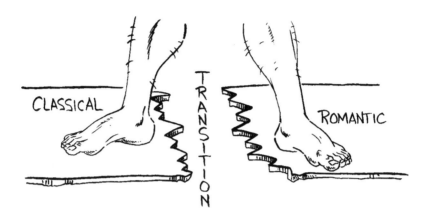

BEETHOVEN STRADDLING HIS PERIODS.

Now, at this point, dear reader, I have a confession to make. The dear Maestro, Colli, i.e. and I have worked together so closely over the years that I've just heard his somewhat gruff and ever-probing voice shouting:

"Are you sticking to the point? This is a book about the piano already, in case you've forgotten and you know your tendency to veer – and this should not be a 'treatise long' but a succinct hard-hitting book that tells the truth about this great instrument and the reader doesn't want to dally."

I tell you, dear reader, the intellectual/spiritual/musical/literary/psychological connection between Colli and me is so real it's sometimes scary. But he's right! And I'm reminded that the title of this chapter is *Busted Wires and Broken Movements* – that is, Beethoven in the later period – and I am about to unravel the mystery that has been plaguing your collective minds since you started reading this chapter.

First, let's look at his BUSTED WIRES!

Here's a new Broadwood Piano, the day it arrived at Beethoven's flat:

BEETHOVEN'S BROADWOOD PIANO (NEW)

Here's that very same Broadwood piano a mere three weeks later, having been used by Beethoven to compose some more of his wonderful opuses – or op-i, as the pedants would have it.

BEETHOVEN'S BROADWOOD PIANO (3 WEEKS LATER.)

A TOTALLY USELESS BUNCH OF BUSTED WIRES! All the strings of the Broadwood were hopelessly busted and he had to write the company and order a new one.

And the reason(s) for this dramatic destruction of an expensive instrument, you ask?

The answers are complex and manifold, but forthcoming.

Busted Wires – Reasons:

1. OK, he was going deaf! One of the great tragedies of Beethoven's life was his gradual descent into aural silence. The collection of earpieces used by the great musical titan look like a display table at Madame Tussaud's museum of ancient gynecological instruments of torture. He'd shoved more things in his ear hole in order to try to hear better than Phyllida Phrank has knitted toilet paper covers for sale at the Chezlee Ont Parsnip and Arts Fest. So he banged on the keys to try to hear better, but ...

b) The construction of the piano had not yet had the advantage of the iron frame and so the strings simply could not withstand Ludwig's pounding in order to try to hear what he was playing slash composing.

(iii) The music he was hearing in his mind as he moved from his early to his "later" period was BIG MUSIC and I mean that in all ways – conceptually as well as dynamically. Like all great visionary artists, he was writing music far beyond the capacity of the instruments he was limited to at his time. He was writing for the piano of the future, which is why he busted the pianos of his day.

4. He never seemed to be able to "make it with the ladies." He never seemed to have a girlfriend or a wife, and whoever "the immortal beloved" was, not even the movie was certain for sure. Now, I don't know about you, dear pursuer of the musical arts, but, and I'm going to be bold and daring here, and just state it shamelessly and forcefully, but when I'm not getting it, I tend to bang on my instrument harder then when I am in the contented raptures of an "after," or an "après" as the French say. Now, if Beethoven was *never* successful in the area of relationships, can you imagine the buildup over the years? No wonder he had a crisis in the middle that changed his periods from early to late and made him change from a Classical composer into a Romantic composer. (And remember, Romantic has nothing to do with sex! But not getting it has a lot to do with how hard you play and can result in busted wires if your construction isn't great and you don't have an iron frame.)

We move on ... to ...

Broken Movements – Reasons:

1. The 18th century was Very Organized!
"How dare you, you dairy dilettante, have the effrontery to make a sweeping generalization like that!?" I can hear echoing through the corridors of your mind as you read that last statement! And I have one word to say to you, and that is "COLLI." That the 18th century was very organized is a direct quote from that mighty titan of the magesterium of musicological knowledge who, when he makes a "sweeper" like that, is able to back it up with a veritable plethora of facts. I, however, will present just a few:

1) Science and the scientific method was being discovered.

2) Philosophers and great thinkers replaced the absolute monarchs of the 17th century and the philosophers and great thinkers have very tidy and organized minds.

c) The Doctrine of Affections was in effect, which meant that each work of art and each part of each work of art had to have a certain or the same affect – and if that isn't organized, I don't know what is.

iv) A variety of forms, developed throughout the 17th century, became FORMALIZED in the later Baroque period, 1700 and on, and while things became a little FLUFFY during the Rococo period, it soon led to the Formal Principles of Classicism, with your Symphony and Sonatas by the score, all with strict, formal and organized rules for how many movements a sonata should have and how each movement should be structured.

5) They were even trying to organize Mother Nature. Even gardens were organized in the 18th century, with shrubs and trees cut and trimmed into geometrical patterns.

vi) need I say more?

g) honestly now, I ask you....

SO WHAT HAPPENED?????

Beethoven, as well as busting his wires, started Breaking his Movements.

The formal, organized structure of the Classical period Beethoven started to change, break down, develop and not follow the rules. This is nowhere more evident than in the great collection of 32 piano sonatas that Beethoven wrote.

Here you see Beethoven's life in a nutshell. You see sonatas of the early period that are ALL STRICT AND FORMAL AND ORGANIZED. And then you see sonatas of the later period
- that don't follow the rules
- in which movements change styles
- that sometimes have only two movements in a sonata
(Shocking!).

In other words, he BROKE THE MOLD and started trying new things, going in new directions. As a result, MUSIC IN GENERAL and PIANO MUSIC SPECIFICALLY would never be the same after Beethoven. And if you want to have anything to do with the PIANO, you must LISTEN TO and LOOK AT

The mighty 32 Beethoven piano sonatas.

(And don't say you love his 5th because he wrote five piano concerti, nine symphonies and who knows? you could mean bourbon. So be specific:

"I love Beethoven's 5th *Piano Sonata!*"

Although No. 5 is just an average one, altho' his 5th piano concerto is brilliant and his 5th symphony (the one that starts da-da-da-*dum*) is his most famous. Just don't go around saying composers' names and a number because the connoiseurs will query justifiably as to "Which 5th?".

The other important thing to remember about Beethoven is that he was a damn fine pianist and performed most of what he wrote himself, so no matter how hard the music is technically it is always thoroughly PLAYABLE. It's written for eight fingers and two thumbs and CAN be played on the piano! This is not always the case, as we'll soon discover. When it came to the piano, Beethoven knew what he was doing, SO REJOICE!

Chapter 10:
"Could we please discuss the Romantics
without mentioning s-e-x?"

Get ready! Pour yourself a good stiff Stoney Ripple double and prepare for a mental flushing! I don't know what era or period of music has been more misunderstood, misrepresented and in general mistaken as the Romantic period.

Romanticism as a movement and a period in artistic history is as much maligned as what goes on here in Obsuria amongst Lucetta, the Maestro and yours truly. The residents of Chezlee Ont seem to take great delight in manufacturing implications and innuendo, winks and nods, nudges and whispers and sometimes even outright 'double entendres' about us that really hurt and upset us. And for the record, I feel impelled as I begin this challenging and controversial chapter to further reveal to you, dear trusted readers who have virtually become close friends, intellectual associates and confidantes, what really goes on between us here in Obscuria. Here 'tis:

1. An intellectual interflow of ideas and opinions that enriches each of our minds. It's a kind of Socratic ménage à trois that's purely Platonic, although personal and caring.

2. We each share responsibilities of the domestic necessities of life and the needs of our agrarian setting like stall-mucking, asparagus stalk shredding and sow bathing.

3. Sadly, I do confess that Lucetta does get burdened with the bulk of the hard labor, as Colli and I are so often involved in musicological or compositional or pedagogical pursuits that a dried teat on Clarice is not something we can interrupt a fugal anaysis for.

4. Lucetta is compensated by the high regard in which we hold her and she does get free tickets to all our concerts and lectures so neither of us feels terribly guilty about the sometimes uneven distribution of chores.

5. Lucetta has just reminded me that she also does windows annually, rutabaga chips bi-annually and pickled preserves in the late summer months so I've made a note to myself to give her a nice pound of that cheese I like so much as a "bijou" gift in appreciation of her efforts.

6. There is NOTHING ELSE going on here amongst or between any of us and the thought of it never occurs to any of us as we wallow and, nay, overindulge in the delights of purely aesthetic intercourse and trialogue. **

** And I hope that puts to rest those vicious rumours that you – Ona Marveen Troope – and yes I name you specifically! – have been circulating about us for years just because I wouldn't dance with you at the United Methodist's Gooseberry Social and you found out it was because I said you had halitosis.

While the piano was born during the Rococo period and went through puberty in the Classical period, it was the Romantic period that saw the teenage wild rebellion move into full adult maturity of the music for piano. And before we look at the wonderful array of Romantic composers who wrote what remains as the bulk of piano music, it is necessary to get the generalities cleared up and understood before we hit the specifics.

First, it's important to understand "Romanticism" in contrast to the Classicism that preceded it, for while the Classic/Romantic or Formal/Expressive aspects of art and music have existed since time immemorial down through the ages, these two specific periods, 1750-1825 and 1825-1900, have unique qualities that separate them from the ongoing Apollonian/Dionysian swing of things. And, as usual, following Colli's advice, a chart would help immensely here to elucidate the understanding.

Study the following chart for a considerable amount of time. As a matter of fact I'm going to give you a series of charts, at the end of which your grasp of the Romantic will be greatly expanded:

Classical Period	*Romantic Period*
- 1750 (roughly)-1825 (or 6)	- 1825 (or 6) – 1900 (approx.)
- Apollo, god of light & measure	- Dionysius – god of intoxication & passion
- tea	- gin
- no sex except for procreation	- no holds barred, you name it
- moderation	- uninhibited, over the top
- beauty within bounds	- beauty without bounds
- objective	- subjective

- impersonal	- personal
- aristocratic	- democratic
- Yeah Greeks!	- Yeah Dark Ages and Gothics!
- organized formal gardens	- let nature go wild
- formal, serious, structured	- fanciful, picturesque, passionate
- Kings, Queens and Aristocrats	- Presidents, Prime Ministers and more Queens
- we've arrived and have all the answers, thank you very much	- we're longing for the possibility of a dream,which is probably non-existent
- God is in HEAVEN	- where is God?
- God is a Man	- all artists are Gods!
- poise	- no poise
- familiar	- strange
- control	- ecstasy
- sane	- nuts
- knowable	- unknowable
- attainable	- unattainable
- the same	- different
- screw the poor	- the oppressed have rights
- Teutonic	- Bohemian
- proper	- shocking
- content	- longing
- certain	- doubtful
- normal	- macabre & eerie
- sober	- drunk

Names of Pieces for the Piano

Classical	Romantic
Sonatina 1	- *Impromptu*
2	- *Moments Musicaux*
3	- *Marche Militaire*
4	- *Polonaise*
etc.	- *Scherzo*
	- *Waltz*
Sonata 1	- *Prelude*
2	- *Etude*
3	- *Papillons*
4	- *Fantasy Pieces*
etc.	- *Romances*

Suite	1	- *Songs without Words*
	2	- *Songs with Words*
	3	- *Songs from Childhood*
	4	- *The Prophet Bird*
	etc.	- *Hungarian Rhapsodies*

Concerto	1	- *Arabesque*
	2	- *Spring Song*
	3	- *Dreams*
	4	- *Nocturne*
	etc.	- *Liebesträume*
		- *Barcarolle*

Kinds of Directions You See Printed at the Top of the Page in Piano Music, Indicating How the Piece Should Be Played

Classical	*Romantic*
- *vivace* (like a bat out of Hell)	- *espressivo* (expressively)
	- *trionfale* (I won!)
- *molto allegro* (really fast)	- *dolce* (sweetly)
	- *misto* (sad but dry)
- *allegro* (fast)	- *cantabile* (songful)
	- *maestoso* (like a queen or king)
- *allegretto* (not so fast)	- *pastorale* (like shepherds & nymphs or your minister if he's not a yeller)
- *moderato* (smack dabin the M.O.R.)	- *con passione* (sexy)
	- *agigato* (cycle 3 on the washing machine)
- *andantino* (rather slowly)	- *religioso* (really boring)
- *andante* (slowly)	- *lamentoso* (crying)
- *largo* (dead slow)	- *dolente* (really crying)
	- *giocoso* (really happy)
	- *con amore* (with love!)
	- *con fuoco* (with fire!)
	- *grave* (like a funeral)
	- *funerale* (like at a funeral)
	- *troppo libido* (too much sex)
	- *celibatione* (no sex)

Now, if that doesn't give you a whiff and a sniff of what the Romantic period was about, I don't know what will.

The second point I must make here is that

I LOVE THE ROMANTIC PERIOD

(and I'm talking artistically, musically, of course)

AND I'M NOT ASHAMED TO ADMIT IT.

The point I'm raising here is that so many people, and particularly some musicologists and scholars, PUT DOWN Romanticism. How shocked I was to discover as I looked up Romanticism in as reputable a reference text as Willi Apel's *Harvard Dictionary of Music* – supposedly an academic, intellectual objective, scholarly reference dictionary – to find the following – and I quote:

"It is a COMMON experience that the APPEAL of MUCH truly Romantic music (Schumann, Chopin, Liszt) WEARS OUT RATHER QUICKLY UPON REPEATED LISTENING, while the greatest works of the Romantic era are ... such as the symphonies of Brahms and Bruckner. Shortly after 1900 there began a reaction against Romanticism which has continuously gained impetus."

The Harvard Dictionary goes on to say that Debussy simply supplanted the "Teutonic" elements of Romanticism with a "Gallic Romanticism" (I'm getting so steamed up here with these quotes that my glasses are fogging ... just a moment ... there ... that's better.)

Willi Apel goes on to start the next paragraph with "In spite of all its LIMITATIONS ..."

Ladies and gentlemen, I can quote no further. Do you believe it? Such an incredible prejudice boldly stated in a formerly respected reference masterpiece?

Do you see why I stated earlier that I love Romantic music and I'm not ashamed of it? Now, to be honest, if I were perhaps faced with a desert-island alternative, I would take

Bach's *Prelude in B-flat minor* from *Book I* of the *Well-Tempered Clavier* rather than any of Mendelssohn's *Songs Without* (or *With*) *Words*. But to put down an entire period with such arrogant disdain breaks the scholarly oath that all bona fide musicologists take – namely to be OBJECTIVE and not allow themselves to be influenced by the particular subjective taste of their particular age or decade or socio-economical group. You can't even say that time will sort it all out as to who's great and who's not. Read a music history textbook printed in Germany between 1939 and 1945 and look up Mendelssohn and you get something like this:

"Der war auch ein jüdische Komponist – Mendelssohn" ("There was also a Jewish composer, Mendelssohn.") and that's it. And we all know why that was ...!

So I boldly proceed, in love and appreciation. But it's a big and productive period, so we can only skim!

Skimming over the Romantic Biggies:
Early Ones
- Beethoven Part II or Second ½, he starts to go Romantic
- Weber (notice only 1 'b' and no relation to the super-rich Sir Andrew Lloyd)
- Schubert – although called a Viennese classicist, he has his feet firmly set in both camps

Full-Blown Romantics
- Berlioz, Mendelssohn, Schumann, Chopin, Liszt, Wagner

Later Ones
- Franck, Bruckner, Brahms, Tchaikovsky (neo-classicists)

Post-Romantics
- Elgar, MacDowell, Reger, Richard Strauss, Sibelius, Holst

We move now specifically to the PIANO and the ROMANTICS and here we have a hot combo. In many senses, the piano was *thee* instrument of the Romantic period, giving rise to the star performers and expressively individualistic compositions. As the composers and performers of this period are generally well known, your humble servant here will give only overviews and tidbits, hoping to spur you on to research the rest of the details yourself, 'cause I just don't have the time. It's furrowing season and I'm working this farm alone here this year, what with the Maestro off doing his musico-dental research.

Now, I don't want you to think that I resent having to do solo furrowing while he's off in Arkansas and I have to cut down on some of the detail in MY book. I don't resent him one bit and Lucetta is helpful when the oxen tire. So it's not that bad. But if it's a comprehensive survey you're looking for, go to the stacks of your local university library and ask for the special pass to floor 7 (lower) and there's tons of stuff there.

OVERVIEWS & TIDBITS ON THE PIANO AND THE ROMANTICS

Berlioz
- played only the guitar
- wrote big works for orchestra, choirs, etc.
- major work (*Symphonie Fantastique*) is about a guy O.D.-ing on opium. Wrote it 'cause he (Berlioz) was smitten with an Irish actress called Harriet Smithson as a kind of adoration/condemnation of her.
- they later met, married, were unhappy and separated
- he seems to have ignored the piano

Schumann
- a journalist/concert pianist
- bunged up his fingers through trying to develop more strength and speed and went bonkers
- wrote tons of wonderful music for the piano but it is TECHNICALLY DIFFICULT. His wife, CLARA, however, practised real hard after he died, performed his works (and HERS as well) all over Europe and made him famous. If you're *really* good and practise *really* hard, you *could* become a Schumann specialist, but few have.

Mendelssohn
- generally knocked by the musicological intelligentsia as not being all that great, but ...
- a child prodigy pianist like Mozart
- overwhelmed by Bach and wrote preludes and fugues and oratorios
- tons of Romantic little ditties called *Songs Without Words* that were reasonably easy to play and became quite popular for the "average" pianists of the 19th century. He was also a close personal friend of "Vicky and Albert" – the Queen (and Prince) of England. And there you have it – the words that bring disdain to musicologists brows. "Easy", "popular", "average" and "friend of Queen Victoria".

- he was ethnically Jewish but described by a Rev. Lampadius two years after his death in 1849 as an Evangelical Christian in the true sense of the word
- now there's a combination! Try a *Song Without Words* anyway – they're not long

Chopin

- the next one in line after BACH, MOZART and BEETHOVEN as MAJOR CONTRIBUTORS TO PIANO LITERATURE and a MUST STUDY FOR ALL WANNABE PIANISTS
- his girlfriend wore men's suits, smoked cigars and called herself George, and he wore a brand-new pair of white gloves every single day of his life, so take that where you will
- Chopin specialists who are brilliant are as common in the piano performance world as black flies are in Bognor's Swamp in August
- wrote tons of piano music that is virtually all GREAT!
- was very privé and never gave a public concert – just private soirée concerts in the "better" homes of Paris
- the reason he doesn't get more space at this time is that he's so well known and loved, I didn't want to re-iterate

Liszt

- thee GREATEST PIANO VIRTUOSO of the 19th century – and he knew it!
- with grand gestures would take off his ever-present white gloves and give a recital, sometimes on two grand pianos, running from one to the other so both sides of the house would see his "amazing" technique
- Liberace could not have studied with him, but must have taken notes.

FRED AND GEORGE

- sometimes ladies and even men would SWOON and/or try to grab articles of clothing as a "divine" memento of a concert.

- he wrote and performed a lot of transcriptions of opera arias that were popular in his day. The audiences (THEN) simply adored them but audiences (NOW) rarely hear them and if they do aren't nearly so impressed, 'cause we can listen to the original on a CD. Technically, only Liszt and a very few others can play most of his piano music 'cause it's so damn difficult. How oft I, myself, have given up

A PICTURE OF LISZT AFTER A RECITAL WHEN WOMEN (AND EVEN MEN) HAD TRIED TO GRAB ARTICLES OF CLOTHING FROM HIS 'DIVINE' PERSON.

in despair in the second bar of a Liszt opus. So bully for those who make it to the end.

- He was a PROLIFIC and SIGNIFICANT COMPOSER albeit, but he did have problems with women, his first liaison was with a woman who wrote under the name DANIEL (cf. Chopin's George) and his next major relationship was with Princess Caroline Sayne-Wittgenstein, who told him to stop playing the piano and write big works. Well, he did and 'cause she'd made a pre-nuptial agreement she got all his manuscripts when he died and then passed them on to her daughter, not of the same name, Princess Marie Hohenlohe-Schillingsfürst, who did found the Liszt Museum and they're publishing all his works and I think they're up to about volume 40 by now if they haven't finished completely. He wrote a lot and a lot of it was really big!

Wagner
- wrote operas
- has to be dealt with in a book of his own

- see *Special-Needs Composers*, coming out in the fall of 2003 (God willing and the crick don't rise).

Elgar, MacDowell, Reger, Richard Strauss, Sibelius, Holst
The only other Romantic I've got space left to deal with is...

Brahms

- was in love with Clara Schumann but even after Robert died she wouldn't marry him, yet in spite (or because) of this, he played the piano brilliantly and wrote a ton of piano music and became the next in line of the biggies – as in BACH, BEETHOVEN, MOZART, CHOPIN, BRAHMS

- he's a bit controversial as some find him a bit of a boring too-Classical Romantic

- others find him totally Romantic, profoundly deep and superbly inventive. So take your pick, but pianistically remember he's significant.

JUST A FEW MORE FACTS TO TIE UP THE ROMANTICS:

1. Composers who could play the piano really well tend to write playable piano music. Composers who don't, tend not to. I think you'll find this to be true.

2. Just as in life, a steady diet of "romancin' " or Romantic music can get exhausting after a while and even lose the excitement and thrill it once had. But, if you vary your piano diet with a bit of Baroque (Bach), a dash of Classical (Mozart & early Beethoven), and a main course of ANY of the Romantics, you will have a cordon-bleu meal of musical delight, particularly if you top it off with a dessert mélange of Debussy, slices of Satie, cream puffs of Poulenc and, instead of cappuccino and a cigar, try a bit of Cage for something different.

3. Be careful what you read about the Romantic composers. Remember *The Harvard Dictionary of Music*? Well, if Thee Harvard can fall into subjective personal bias, WHO CAN'T ??? So always sort out your FACTS from your OPINIONS and ferret out those little prejudices just like a Jack Russell sniffing out tree stumps for rats. Make up your own mind: That's all I have to say about that.

4. I love it! Romantic music for the piano is a delight to play and a pleasure to hear. Enjoy!

Chapter 11:
The Truth Revealed: "You can't play a whole note on the piano," sez Debussy

Perhaps one of the major reasons neither Colli nor I (nor even Lucetta, for that matter) gets invitations to the purely social events in Chezlee Ont is essentially because of our well-earned reputation for speaking the truth. The local mavens of society – "Les Grandes Dames de Chezlee" – are, and I must say with some justification, squeamish about including us in a "cucumber sandwich and tea" or a "duck àl' orange soirée" because, God knows, if asked, we will respond honestly and betimes with that kind of probing truthfulness that can curdle the cream or cause a crumpet to fall from a delicate hand.

And I must say, without mentioning the details, that the cultural community of Chezlee Ont has not yet recovered from Lucetta's remark at the Squiffleford's French Fête last June, or what the Maestro said at Madge and Pearl Thackenberry's Summer Solstice Jam-bourée when asked (by Pearl herself) to comment on why great artists paint "all those nude people." Idle gossip is not the purvue of this book, but needless to say there is a price to be paid for the kind of brutal honesty that we (the Maestro, Lucetta and I) are committed to.

We do, however, have the great joy of that sense of identification with the "truly greats" in history who have also dared to walk that same path and proclaim the Emperor to be stark raving naked! And here of course we identify with that Mother of Modern Music, M. Claude Achilles Debussy when he shocked the entire musical world and pianists and composers specifically when he said (and I translate roughly from French):

"Ya can't play a whole note on the piano!"
– Claude Achilles Debussy
(Fri. morning circa 10:27 a.m., late 19th c.)

Dear reader, I know how shocking this revelation is so
a)   sit
b)   breathe heavily
c)   repeat the mantra – "Brahms is boring" – 11 times
d)   have a Coke!

There now, aren't you better? Now let me gently explain EXACTLY WHAT DEBUSSY MEANT!

When you SING a whole note, you can hold it for a relatively long time

LAAAAAAAAAAAAAAAAAAAAAAAH
(singing a whole note for a long time)

When you play a whole note on a wind or brass instrument, it lasts as long as your breath does

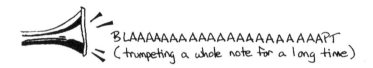

BLAAAAAAAAAAAAAAAAAAAAAAAAPT
(trumpeting a whole note for a long time)

When a string player plays a whole note, it lasts as long as you can drag that bow over the string

MMMMMMMMMMMMMMMMMMMM
(stringing a whole note for a long time)

BUT
When a pianist strikes a key to play what is written as a whole note, look what happens:

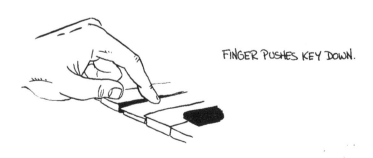

FINGER PUSHES KEY DOWN.

3. and even with the damper pedal down so that no dampers stop the sound,
> THAT STRING CAN VIBRATE ONLY FOR SO LONG!
> THE SOUND QUICKLY DIES. THERE'S NO
> AIR THAT KEEPS BLOWING
> ARM THAT KEEPS BOWING
> ARMS THAT KEEP RATTLING
> NOTHING MORE HAPPENS!!
> THE SOUND DIES!!

As a matter of fact, every single note on the piano, whether
whole note, half note, quarter note, whatever note, DIES AND
DIMINISHES RAPIDLY IN SOUND like

a) a gunshot whose sound reverberates briefly but is soon
gone

b) certain bodily organs, particularly male ones, which
having performed one of the functions for which they were in-
tended immediately fade and whither, fall limp and die. (And
mentioning this particular example is why I've never been asked
back to the First Baptist Church Bible Study and Butter Tart
Night held every third Thursday during Lent – and I did enjoy
the Baptist's tarts!)

c) a lot of things that go off like a cannon and quickly disappear

Is Debussy's point penetrating the inner recesses of your musical mind? Are the shocking implications of what he said reverberating down the anals of your collective crania? Are you reeling? Because you should be!

A piece of piano music might look like this:

But that same piece of music probably SOUNDS more like this:

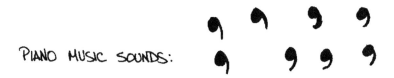

Now, I hope you've got this point because we need to move on to the question that I know is eating away in the minds of all you intellectually bright lights out there – namely

SO WHAT???

or perhaps, more prudently put:

What are the implications of Debussy's statement: "Ya can't play a whole note on the piano!"?

They are twofold and intellectually mind-blowing, so fasten your cerebral seat belts and prepare for take off.

1. Implication A

Composers had to become MORE HONEST when they wrote MUSIC FOR THE PIANO and take into account that the piano is a percussion instrument in which once the note is struck, the sound DIES AWAY never to be sustained or revived. Therefore, the way to notate piano music started to change with Debussy and many after him followed in his fashion.

2. Implication B

The amazing thing is that in spite of the fact that you can't really play a whole note and the sound is always dying – YOU CAN STILL CREATE THE ILLUSION THAT YOU'RE PLAYING WHOLE NOTES AND THE SOUND ISN'T DYING AWAY.

One of the reasons this is true is that it took 400 years of keyboard writing and playing before Debussy discovered it. If it was so obvious, somebody would have realized it sooner. The fact that they didn't means that pianists were PRETTY DARN GOOD AT CREATING THE ILLUSION THAT THE SOUND WASN'T DYING ALL THE TIME.

Do you see what I mean? Perhaps a diagram will assist!

Here's a melody in whole notes that could be sung, played on a cello, blown on a tuba etc.:

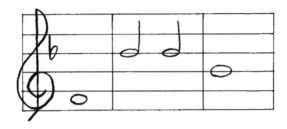

Look at what happens to that same melody played on the piano:

As soon as the sound is made, it starts dying away!

YET WHEN A GOOD PIANIST PLAYS THAT MELODY, YOU GET THE IMPRESSION THEY'RE PLAYING WHAT'S WRITTEN (i.e. whole notes and half notes).

For the secret of how to play the piano and give the IMPRESSION that the notes aren't always dying and you're playing a sustained melodic line, phone me here at Obscuria at Chezlee 2-0022 and arrange for a 10-week course called "Weaving Magic at the Keyboard." My rates are cheap considering I'm damn good and I sometimes accept payment in kind depending on the kind ...

But, getting back to Debussy,

As you learned in one or another of my other books, he was

the Mother of Modern Music and his numerous works for the piano are no small part of his revolutionary change from Romantic to Modern.

First of all, let me say that in our growing list of piano "musts," he must be added. He played the piano and wrote well for it, so slap him down!

Bach, Mozart, Beethoven, Chopin, Brahms, Debussy: A steady diet of these and you will be a well-tempered pianist.

France was a hotbed of cultural activity during Debussy's time and Paris was the centre of it. In art, the Impressionists were painting up a revolutionary storm and Debussy was influenced heavily by what the Impressionists were saying and painting.

Do you remember the difference between what pieces for the piano were called in the Classical and then the Romantic periods? Well, just get a load in a page or two of the titles of some of the pieces from this period of music when Romanticism was boiling up and over and composers were looking for new ideas.

And Debussy was not alone. Satie and Ravel were also writing wonderfully imaginative works that should be added to any decent pianist's repertoire. Satie died owning several hundred umbrellas and 12 unworn three-piece corduroy suits. Ravel had the hugest clock collection around and in most of his pieces you hear tic-ing *and* toc-ing going on somewhere and he went a bit bonkers at the end hearing a high B-flat on a piccolo – not nice to hear on anything, but the piccolo can be really obnoxious.

This period of the sunset years of the 19th century into the 20th century is called the ...

FIN DE SIÈCLE (End of the Century)

or

L'Age d'Or (The Golden Age)

And there is a wild, woolly, wealth of works from this period that provide ample fodder for the thirsty piano learner. Here's another skimmy list of guys worth looking up:

Fauré	*Scriabin*	*Elgar*
Franck	*Janacek*	*Delius*
Dukas	*Respighi*	*Holst*
Roussel	*Albeniz*	*Vaughn Williams*

There are tons more! Most of them wrote music for the piano! Look 'em up! Listen to 'em! And enjoy!

Titles of Pieces for the Piano in the Impressionist Age of the Fin de Siècle or *L'Age d'Or:*

The Girl with the Flaxen Hair
The Sunken Cathedral
The Little Negro
Golliwog's Cake Walk
Three Pieces in the Shape of a Pear
Gymnopédie (?)
Children's Corner
Dr. Gradus ad Parnassum
Light of the Moon (or Moonlight)
Water Games
Reflections in the Water
Goldfish
Ondine
Mirrors
States of Soul
Poem of Fire
Poem of Ecstasy
The Divine Poem
The Satanic Poem
White Mass
Black Mass
Dreams
Masks
The Island of Joy
In Black and White
The Heroic Lullaby to render homage to S.M. King
      Albert I of Belgium and to his Soldiers!

Does this list give you an idea of how things were changing?

Chapter 12:
Fondled, Slapped, Kicked and Tickled: The piano advances (?) into the 20th Century

While I have lauded and applauded the stimulating intellectual slash cultural milieu of our petite bucolic community known as Chezlee Ont, there is a SEEDIER SIDE to our platonic bliss. I suppose every town has it, just as every family has at least one skeletal member. And, like the good page who marked the footsteps of King Wenceslaus, I too tread in those massive prints left by that great musicological trodder – Colli Albani, who was and is never afraid to face the bold truth and expose it for what it is and get on with it.

So – boldly going where he (the Maestro) has gone before, I state:

1. Chezlee Ont has a Massage Parlor

2. It is run by Merle Rutt and employs a number of girls from down on the east side and a few from Grousetown – out Kimble way

3. Last Sunday, during a really tedious section of Rev. McDudd's sermon series on "the use of the word 'the' in the writings of the minor prophets," I dashed the following note

off to my friend G.D. Phineas, sitting in the pew in front of Lucetta and me.

4. "G.D. – YOU LOOK SOOOOO RELAXED! Have you been to Merle's for Massage?

5. Four minutes later, just as the Rev. was finally concluding about the final "the" in the book of Amos, I received the following note pressed in the Presbyterian Hymnal (Revised) (between 455 (*How great a Salvation*) and 456 (*He Touched Me, Ohhhhh He Touched Me*)

"Dear A. E. How perceptive!
Not only was I massaged!
I was FONDLED, SLAPPED, KICKED
And
TICKLED!!!

"All rise and sing hymn number 737 – *Yield not to temptation, for yielding is sin.*" Rev. McDudd's voice boomed out, the substitute organist began, but you know my mind was not on the singing of that hymn. I was put in mind of how aptly that description of G. D.'s time at Merle's Massage Parlor would be the perfect title for this chapter – namely – the piano moves into the 20th century.

I cannot tell you how relieved I've been since Jan 1, 2000 when we can finally talk ABOUT the 20th century. It's like those times you've been at a meeting – like for example the planning meeting of the Chezlee Ont Annual Parsnip and Arts Festival – and Wilma Frye comes. We can all barely wait until she goes to the Women's Institute W.C. to talk about her. Her fashion sense is somewhere between a Bedouin nomad and a mad Druid priest and her teeth ...! But enough of that.

My point is that we are now FREE to discuss the 20th century because we're in the 21st century. Granted, we only have, at present writing, a few months' perspective, but we can at least speak openly, freely, generally and overviewingly about the 20th without getting into trouble.

The period we call MODERN – from 1900 to 1999 – was a very exploratory time when composers felt it necessary to

1. TRY ANYTHING ONCE and
2. NEVER REPEAT ANYTHING TWICE

This modern principle was applied not only to composition but to the instruments themselves on which these modern compositions were performed. Composers, moving from Debussy's dictum that you can't play a whole note on the piano, started doing all sorts of things to the instrument, of which "fondled, slapped, kicked and tickled" are mere tips of the icebergs of abuse the poor piano has suffered throughout our recent century.

The piano has not been singled out to be picked on. Far from it! Here are some of the obscene things I've seen done with instruments during the performance of a "modern" piece of music:

THINGS I'VE SEEN DONE:

a) A double bass turned round backwards and thumped like a tom-tom

B) A violin bow thwapped on the wooden brace holding the strings

3) A pianist stretched inside his grand, dropping kitchen cup fasteners on the strings

iv) A brick dropped on the concert hall parquet floor

e) A cello bow drawn through a bamboo bird cage

6) The keys of a saxophone slapped sans blowing

Now, don't get me wrong! There has been a mainstream of decent composers, still looking at the piano as a pretty damn good instrument and writing perfectly legitimate pieces to be PLAYED on the piano with the thumbs and fingers God gave us.

Perhaps I'm overly sensitive about the "modern" use of the piano because I'm still working my butt off to pay Miss P. Wilda Widgeon back for the destruction of her lovely Bösendorfer concert grand piano that got chopped to bits by an axe when the Maestro performed John Cage's work for soprano, piano and axe, and I'm going to be pushing up daisies before I'm finished paying Wilda back, so you see why I'm a little uptight!

There has been a certain school of music throughout the 20th century one can only describe as

THE DESTRUCTIVE SCHOOL OF MUSIC

And the piano itself as well as the music written for it has suffered from much of the abuse of this period.

The other problem with piano music in the 20th century, even among the less radical composers of piano literature, has been the overwhelming influence of the

AMERICAN SCHOOL OF PIANO PLAYING

I will discuss the various schools in later chapters under these headings:

A. The Russian/English Method
2. The French Way
iii) ... Americans! ...

However, let me say here, in this chapter, that – just as New York has adopted belting as "thee" way to sing ever since Ethel sang the way she did and she couldn't help it – so the Americans have said:

1. Thuh pianah's ah percussive instrument
2. Don't matter none how ya push them little keys down, that hammer still hits them keys thuh same way
3. So bang bang bang away. Tone quality is *no* different so bang away.

Needless to say, this American attitude has produced music that sounds like it comes from a shingle factory and pianists who ought better to be employed in an abattoir or butcher's shop.

Where we stand now, in the present age, teetering on the very precipice of the 21st century, just catching our breath to gaze back at the 20th century, GOD KNOWS! As we live in a very pluralistic age (see somewhere in my last book under *Pluralism is not Polygamy*), there are many situations in which the piano and pianists find themselves. And as Lucetta has just read this last bit over my shoulder and said "Ya know what Colli would have said – Give' em a list" – and so – I will.

WHERE THE PIANO AND PIANISTS FIND IT AND THEMSELVES TODAY:

1. Nice people still play nice piano music written by nice dead people all over the world
ii) Nice people still play nice piano music written by nice people who are still alive, all over the world
c) Some people still fondle, slap, kick and tickle the devil out of the piano and call it modern (altho' it's really quite old) and usually there's only three people in the audience – the composer, her husband and her mother
(they usually don't allow dogs in concert halls so Fido couldn't come)
4. Yanni still plays the C-major scale up and down (usually just the first six notes) and gets paid too much money and the women all sigh and go "Ooooooooooh?"

     e) Rock and Rollers use synthesizers and refer to a real piano as "An acoustic?"

     vi) Church basements, legions, seniors' residences and all three of my aunts all have huge old upright Heintzman pianos that were once very good but are now so out of tune they sound like some of the things that sound like c) – see above

     7) Electric pianos, that are touch sensitive are becoming more and more popular because:

          a) they're cheaper

          b) they don't go out of tune

          c) they are more or less transportable

          d) they have a transposing switch so you can play the same song in any key you like, which makes

Lucetta so much happier, as she can sing *Pale Hands I Loved Beside the Shalimar* in F as she is now virtually a bass, she has dropped so much with age

          e) You can usually get a few other bells and whistles (like harpsichord and organ), which can spruce things up a bit if you're having a soirée and you want to add a bit of Baroque.

     I realize that hitherto I have not mentioned a single pianist, composer of piano music, or anything specific. We have been wallowing in a sea of generalities, understanding principals and paradigms but not mentioning specifics.

     Now as the time marches on, the number of specifics increase up the wazoo, so that to be comprehensive becomes a total impossibility.

     Lucetta has just yelled that there's a grease fire in the kitchen, so you'll have to do your own research to finish this chapter. Sorry. "Coming Lucetta."

Chapter 13:
The Servant, the Diva, the Brain
and the Architect – and others

As I sat down on the old milking stool on the verandah of Obscuria the other night to commence Chapter 13, I must confess I became so overwhelmed with a sense of inadequacy and the loss of the ever-present presence of the Maestro that I sniffled. Just once, mind you, but I did sniffle, wondering how I was going to tackle a chapter on the "Great Pianists" without being able to run it over first with Colli and glean these stimulating insights from his oh-so-informed mind that would spur and prod me on to at least try to attain a level of excellence comparable to his own.

As I sat on my little stool, a sad sigh followed my stifled sniffle and I felt I was about to sob heavily when Lucetta yelled out from the kitchen, where she was preserving kumquats and quince, "I need sugar, lard, salt and whey." And with that list, a mental lightning bolt hit me.

There I'd been, roving back and forth over 300 years of superb pianists wondering how I could ever comprehensively and adequately represent them in the stingy little chapters our publisher allows us, when Lucetta's list hit me. BE SPECIFIC, the message rang out! Discuss three or four and from there the readers will be able to roam themselves, look at lists or listen to discs and they will understand the principles and be able to fill in the details themselves.

And that dear readers is how SUGAR, LARD, SALT and WHEY became the Servant, the Diva, the Brain and the Architect, and I shall discuss them in that order.

But first, a few general minutiae about concert pianists:

GENERAL CONCERT PIANIST MINUTIAE

1. *All* babies are born with what look like long, spindly fingers and are no indication that the child will be a concert pianist.

2. Most, or at least many, of the world's great concert pianists had or have short, stocky fingers.

3. Long, spindly fingers in an adult are, by and large, unwieldy, shaky things that do not produce good technical playing that is solid and secure.

4. Excessive body movement, swaying, mumbling, con-
ducting, singing, conversing, circulating whilst playing is
a) disturbing
b) distracting
c) diverting
d) disconcerting and
e) a damn nuisance.

5. Remember: Other concert artists take their own instruments with them when they give a concert, whether it's a piccolo or a double bass. They always play on the SAME instrument. Concert pianists always have to give their concerts on a
DIFFERENT piano from the one they have at home to practise on. With the exception of Vladimir Horowitz, who at the
apex of his career would truck around his own grand (if he was
performing in North America) but he got paid a bucket, so he
could afford to "tote his own" as it were. (Anton Kuerti usually
does this and he also tunes it, too.)

All other concert pianists have to go to the concert hall early,
check out the local grand and give their recital on an instrument
they're totally unfamiliar with.

Q. Does this put pianists at a disadvantage?

A. You bet your sweet tootsie roll it does.

Q. Does this make concert pianists more
a) jumpy?
b) nervous?
c) fussy?
d) all of the above?

A. You betcha!

So take these practical considerations into account when
considering a concert career. Perhaps you'd be better off as a
concert triangle-ist or a snare drummer 'cause you can "tote
your own."

Now to return to our regular programming and Lucetta's
yell of

"SUGAR! LARD! SALT! and WHEY!"

that became in my mind:

The Servant, the Diva, the Brain and the Architect

How could I possibly cover *all* the pianists other than a comprehensive list with a thumbnail sketch? Boring and pedestrian, I hear you saying, and I agree. Instead we commence a

mystery tour: The Servant, the Diva, the Brain, the Architect. Who are they? Why were they great? What do they represent? And I know there are tons of puzzled queries you have, so why don't we start?

The SERVANT

I'll never forget that night. The Four Square Gospel Hall was packed to the rafters. How the girls of the Parsnip and Arts Fest Central Committee had snagged the famous Artur Rubenstein, I never found out. But snag him they did and precisely at 8 p.m. he made his way onto that humble rural concert stage and sat down at Miss P. Wilda Widgeon's Bösendorfer grand piano (it was long before the performance of the John Cage work for soprano, piano and axe that ended its career – the piano's, that is.)

Rubenstein was 83 at the time and the standing ovation and sustained applause when he entered the hall created such an unbridled rush of expectation that if he had played *Mary Had a Little Lamb* correctly with one hand the applause would have been thunderous. To stay awake for a 2½-hour concert at 83 is an Olympian feat in itself – much less play the concert – much less play the concert BRILLIANTLY. But all of these he did magnificently. And what happened that stellar evening as he performed piece after piece formed the basis of the concept of Rubenstein – The Servant.

Now, I've always had a particular fondness for Artur because of the tremendous sense of identification I have with him. Once, years previously, I heard him in a special lecture discuss the fact that he was a late bloomer, a late starter. He was already in his early 40s when his wife said to him "Why don't you practise, Artur? You could be good, you know!" or something like that.

Well, when I heard that, there was such a warm glow that flooded my entire aesthetic being as I realized how much Artur Rubenstein and Anthon E. Darling had in common. How often have I heard those very words, "Why don't you practise, Anthon?" and "You could be good, you know!" coming both from the Maestro and dear, sweet Lucetta, although, in her case, not always referring to my keyboard skills. And I constantly feel I'm on the verge of blooming, even at my age. So you can understand why I have such a bond with Artur. (Also I have six letters in my first name; he has five; how much symbolically closer can two artists be?)

Anyway, to return to the concert that night that Rubenstein gave at the Four Square Gospel Hall in Chezlee Ont. Each piece he played was a tribute. And it was a tribute to the composer, NOT performer (as in, himself). It was as if he were saying:

"Here's the Chopin *Prelude in D-flat major*, commonly known as *The Raindrop*. Isn't it exquisitely lovely? Didn't Chopin do a wonderful job writing this piece? My God, didn't Chopin have a gift?" Rubenstein totally submerges his own performing ego and the natural desire to put "his own stamp" on the music, and renders for us Chopin – pure unadulterated Chopin! Rubenstein is the SERVANT, Chopin is the MASTER. And of course, at 83, he "brought out" piece after piece as if he were introducing a group of old friends whom he loved and adored. It seemed as he started to play, he was saying: "Here's a dear old friend of mine. I've known and loved her for years. I'm sure you'll love her, too."

Anyway, the point is made and I'm never one to indulge in reiteration or unnecessary redundancy so I won't repeat what I've just said that Artur Rubenstein's brilliance lay in his ability to be a SERVANT, if you will, to the composer, to the music, to the text, and present it pure and uncontaminated, so we and he enjoy it together. Brilliant!

THE DIVA

Around the same time, the Maestro, Lucetta and I headed off down to the "big smoke" for an equally ecstatic evening of pianistic superlatives. The other "biggie" of the 20th century, Vladimir Horowitz, was touring again and giving recitals around the world, including a return to his native Russia. He was 78 or -9 at the time we heard him and, like fine wine, or Lucetta's head cheese, he certainly proved that aging only improves the flavor (except for Lucetta's rutabaga chips, which do go "off" after a year or two.)

Horowitz was staggeringly brilliant. And, as our friend Wilfred Whelston told us, after he'd tuned the Horowitz grand, ONE REASON for the brilliance of the tone quality of his playing was that Horowitz had shellacked his hammers as hard as French polished furniture.

Teaching Detour: The harder the felt hammers are when they strike the string, the more brilliant, sharper, more zesty, more tinkly the tone quality. The softer the felt hammers are when they strike the string, the gentler, richer, velvetier, smoother the tone quality. To make hammers harder, both age and shellac are used. To make hammers softer, an inverted pin cushion is used to break down the hardness.

Although the Horowitz recital was as EQUALLY BRILLIANT as the Rubenstein one, it was diametrically opposed in concept and presentation.

Horowitz's interior dialogue ran something like this: "Remember Beethoven's *Pathétique Sonata*? Well, here's Vladimir's version of it! Isn't it amazing what I'm doing? Did you believe how I played that last motif? Who could imagine what heights I could reach using Beethoven as my launching pad?"

At the end of each number, instead of clapping "Yeah, Chopin and thank you, Artur," it was a case of "Yeah, Vladimir, thank you, Horowitz." Now, don't get me wrong. Both pianists had egos. Both were brilliant masters, both technically and musically superb – the one brilliant as the SERVANT, the other brilliant as the DIVA.

Although, I do confess, being the ultimate of humility itself, I do not find as strong a sense of identification with the artist who says "Aren't I simply too great!" as it does conflict with my Anabaptist/Presbyterian roots. However, Horowitz was unquestionably a superbly brilliant pianist and there are many who follow in his footsteps, putting their own stamp all over Mozart or Schumann or Liszt or whoever, and alas many of them lack the mastery of their master they imitate. You've got to be damn good to be a DIVA! And Horowitz was one of the best.

THE BRAIN

Occasionally, in the course of history, there are certain individuals who come along whose bulb burns brighter than the rest in the package. And when most of us fall into the 40-, 60-, or 100-watt category, there's that one 300-watt that comes along and makes the rest of us look rather dim.

Now, I recognize this type of genius because of my long association, both personal and professional, with that luminous, cephalitic genius known albeit fondly as Maestro Colli Albani.

How often my own dark and murky mind has been lit up by the rays of intelligence that beam forth from his Italianate dome.

It has not therefore been difficult for me to identify Colli's mental equal in the field of piano playing and declare categorically and unanimously that the famous Canadian pianist Glenn Gould is the obvious choice for the great one named the BRAIN.

Not that Gould bypassed the heart or guts when he delved into the mind of his mental equal – namely J.S. Bach. No! His playing is never without feeling. But the structure, the form, the levels of construction are all laid out before us to, if we are able, understand and appreciate. Needless to say, Gould specialized in the Apollonian rather than the Dionysian composers. Bach and Beethoven were favored rather than Gottschalk or Satie. There needed to be a mental mountain for Gould to scale and conquer, a musical Everest he could mount and master. And he did this brilliantly. In some sense he was a Servant, a Diva, a Brain and an Architect all wrapped up in one mighty brain. Sadly, his need for absolute perfection ended his public performing career, shifting him to recording, and his light itself was extinguished far too early. More than any other contemporary pianist, he was able to display the structure, the content and the meaning of the most difficult and cerebral works in the piano repertoire and STILL MAKE MUSIC – music that, while it stimulated the farthest reaches of your cranial activity, still stirred the heart to passions that unfortunately made Gould himself sing in joyful exaltation. Joyful it was. Understandable given the breadth and depth of his understanding. But pleasant to listen to? I think not. His "singing" was atrocious and why he kept doing it even in his recording career is beyond reason. The best explanation, from his own lips, was that an adolescent tic remained too long unchecked and became permanently incorporated and unremovable.

But overwhelmingly forgivable. God knows, we here in Obscuria well know the flaws that come with genius. In fact, if the number of flaws is any way indicative of the extent of the genius, then the Maestro and I are over the moon and Mensabound. We have been called "seriously flawed" so many times that our IQs both individually and collectively must be astronomical. And now the last of the four archetypal types:

THE ARCHITECT

In the great Apollonian/Dionysian swing of music, the 19th century Romantic period is one of the highest expressions of the Dionysian pole. Emotions of Bachanalian heights were unleashed during this Romantic period. Feelings oozed unchecked. The heart was exposed and wrung out for all it was worth. Fantasy was explored to the nth degree. Agony and ecstasy were plumbed and scaled. No holds were barred. Anyway, you get the picture!

But in the midst of all this Romantic maelstrom, there was, however, structure, thought and intelligence. Not perhaps the sheer cranial complexities of the Bach *Goldberg Variations*, but levels and strata that undergirded all that emotional slosh.

Far too often, in the performance of works from the Romantic period – and particularly in the repertoire for the piano of this period – certain – nay, most – concert pianists take us through a bar-by-bar, blow-by-blow, gastroenterital gush of *FEELINGS* that takes these wonderful works and turns them into a kind of emotional toilet bowl, mostly expurgating the performer's angst and neuroses and leaving the audience little to enjoy except for those who get their rocks off watching someone go through therapy.

Whew! I must stop here for a moment 'cause my pressure's gone up and I'll have to have a little sip of Lucetta's serviceberry wine from the summer of '86. That stuff has fermented itself back to the Middle Ages but boy it can sure calm you down quick when you've got riled up about something.

Serviceberry Wine Break!

There, that's much better!

Now, returning to the question at hand – namely – the ARCHITECT. In actual fact, it was the BRAIN (a.k.a. Glenn Gould) who pointed out the ARCHITECT! Yes, it was Glenn himself who said that our friend William Aide was the best ARCHITECT concert pianist there was! And, as Desi used to say so often to Lucy, "Let me 'splain!"

In works of the Romantic period, not only is it good to have an OVERVIEW, it's an absolute must. Otherwise you get so LOST in sheer FEELING, you have no sense of where you are. William Aide always lets you know where you are, even in the midst of the most wild and intense emotional outpouring.

There is always present the architectural blueprint that says, "Remember that last cascading torrent of feeling? And now, even though we're luxuriating in a placid pool of peacefulness, watch out! 'Cause were heading for a cataract slash whitewater rapid section that'll create a *mal de mer* worse than that last waterfall."

Do you see, or rather, hear what I mean, dear reader? No matter the intensity of the turbulence, with William Aide, there is always a road map that gently prevents us from ending up in Pittsburgh when it's Paris we're travelling to. And therein lies Aide's genius.

So there they are! The Servant, the Diva, the Brain, the Architect. Four Musketeers of the Pianoforte. Use them as a springboard. Not all pianists fit into these categories or their opposites. Simply use these as an open-ended paradigm for your own leaping about and leaping off into the pool of pianists that beckons us all. Three of the four I've mentioned are dead, for God's sake, and William has looked old for years. There are new ones coming up. One of them is Evgeny Kissin – a young Russian concert pianist whom we had the privilege of hearing just a few years ago when he was only 19 and the Four Square Gospel Hall was only 1/3 filled. Yet the music we heard that night coming out of those adolescent Slavic fingers bespoke of the magic and maturity of a seasoned artist of the highest calibre.

So listen to 'em. Listen to 'em all. If they sound like crap, say so. And if they're great, stand up and applaud. We need to get MORE excited about EXCELLENCE and MORE upset by CRAP.

Chapter 14:
Whose School are you From???

There are three schools in Chezlee Ont. They are the Sydenburgh Country School, Grades 1 to 13 (or whatever they're calling it nowadays), the St. Veronica's Separate School, Grades 7 to 13 (ditto) and the Beulahland Christian Alternative School, grades 1 to 13 (ditto). And in Chezlee Ont, IT MATTERS GREATLY which school you've come from! It shouldn't, but it does!

The comments I have heard at church socials or municipal lunches regarding certain behavioral patterns that were characterized by remarks like:

a) Of course, what can you expect, she's from Veronica's

b) Beulahland! Beulahland! It's written all over him

c) Thank God we went to Sydenburgh, Emily, otherwise ... you know what I mean...?

d) Etc. et al e.g.

Well, BELIEVE IT OR NOT, schools exist in piano playing and, strangely enough, there are, like in Chezlee Ont, three of them!

They are:

1. The Russian/English School
2. The French School
3. The American School

And I shall discuss them in that order. But first I have to add a small codicil or rider or rather, actually, to be honest, a confession.

I have to confess that I was raised in Number One, namely the Russian/English school. I therefore have a bias – a "point of view" – that does effect my usually purely objective scientific scholarly approach with which I tackle any and every subject, as I am sure you are aware from reading the rest of my books. This is why I feel I must confess to you that in this present topic, personal prejudice does predominate and you will see it demonstrated even in the number of inches each of the schools gets. Having said this, I press on.

The Russian/English School of Piano Playing

One of THEE most important aspects about the learning and teaching of piano playing is pedigree. Who was your teacher?

And who was your teacher's teacher? For in the art of playing the piano, similar to Chinese cuisine, there are "trade secrets" passed down from generation to generation that don't appear in books, especially the *Reader's Digest* condensed books, in spite of what they claim to possess.

And here, if I may be allowed to boast just a bit – although you'd think I'd be a far more famous concert pianist than I am given my lineage – I'd like to outline my lineage, pianistically speaking – Here 'tis:

> *Beethoven*
> taught
> *Czerny*
> who taught
> *Matthay* (England)
> and also taught
> *Leschetizky* (Russia)
> who taught
> *Hayunga Carmen*
> who taught
> *Catherine Baird*
> who taught
> *ME, Prof. Anthon E. Darling*

And there you have it. Descended from Beethoven, the two great pedagogues in 1900 were Tobias Matthay (England) and Theodor Leschetizky (Russia), and as there was an essential unity in their approach to the 88, they became known as the Russian/English School, and as they both were my great-great-grand-teachers, I get it from both sides, as it were, so to speak.

Now I can just hear Colli's voice speaking to me from across the miles where he is down there in southwest Arkansas, saying: "Give them the nut, Anthon, the essence! Don't pile up jargon or pile up useless examples! Give them the principles, the basics. The details they can ferret out themselves later in other books. You want to give them the NUT." (My stars! It's so real when I hear him speaking I almost start talking back to him out loud. I'd better watch that!)

So what is the NUT – the ESSENCE – of the Russian/English school of piano playing, you ask? Well, to sum up the whole business in the pithiest epithet I can find, it would be this:

IT *MATTERS* HOW YOUR FINGER TOUCHES THE KEY AND DEPRESSES IT.

As a matter of fact, it mattered so much to Tobias Matthay that in 1903 he wrote a 328-page book about it called *The Act of Touch*. At the time, scoffers in the press (and are there any other kind??? I ask you!?) called it "one man's fad that will soon disappear"! June 1963 was its 15th printing: hardly a fad! Now, I know I can't get into details but I have to 'splain just a little bit about the essence:

1. The F.A.R.K. principal. This means that the basic position from which all "playing" occurs is with the Fingers Always Resting on the Keys. And they NEVER LOSE CONTACT with the KEYS, as a basic position. When playing quickly or for certain effects they, naturally, do leave the keys but only then to return to the RESTING POSITION.

2. The ACT OF TOUCH – the act of depressing the key – is as follows:

a. THE FINGER PUSHES THE KEY DOWN
b. THE FINGER RELAXES
c. THE KEY PUSHES THE FINGER UP

Just to elucidate point b, the ACTION on an acoustic piano is such that if the FINGER completely RELAXES, the KEY ACTION that returns the key to the normal position after being depressed will PUSH UP THE FINGER TO THE "NORMAL" position of the KEY WITHOUT THE FINGER EVER LOSING CONTACT WITH THE KEY.

3. LOUDNESS in piano playing is achieved through relaxed weight – finger, hand, arm (and more if necessary) – but relaxed weight. Depending on the volume desired, the natural weight of the body parts involved in playing is "DROPPED" into the KEY, ALWAYS IN A RELAXED MANNER. Also called DOWN-TOUCH, it is the principle that if RELAXED WEIGHT is used to depress the key, the tone qualities will never be harsh and abrasive but will always be strong yet resonant.

4. Following in the tradition laid out by Carl Philipp Emanuel Bach that the piano should be a singing instrument, the purpose of steps 1, 2 and 3 is to produce a SINGING, RINGING TONE that allows for the maximum MUSICAL EXPRESSIVENESS. While the piano IS a PERCUSSIVE INSTRUMENT, if it is played properly, it does not have to sound HARSH

or STRIDENT. It matters how you hit it – and there's a nut-shell for you.

5. Last, there mustn't be stiffness or rigidity in joints, par-ticularly the wrist, but they must remain LOOSE and FREE, allowing for maximum flexibility. Occasionally, for certain special effects, a certain FIRMNESS of the wrist or forearm may be temporarily adopted, but once that "special effect" is over, the joints return to that LOOSE, RELAXED POSITION.

Both Matthay and Leschetizky always emphasized the im-portance of TONE QUALITY and MUSICAL EXPRESSIVE-NESS. József Gát in his book called *The Technique of Piano Playing* quotes Imre Ungár:

"It is not the speed of the fingers that is equivalent to good technique: it is the ability to make the piano weep and smile, to evoke human and artistic feelings and manifestations."

How often have I myself, at the end of a frustrating lesson with a recalcitrant "thumping" student, or even at the end of a public recital of a "thumpy" concert pianist, have felt like saying:

"Why don't you buy a Smith Corona and just type the damn piece!"

There is so much more that could be said but you're not paying for a piano lesson so that's all I'll say for now about the Anglo-Russian School.

All I will add is, if you're currently taking piano lessons, ask your teacher what SCHOOL he or she belongs to and if your teacher doesn't know, you could be in trouble.

The French School of Piano Playing

Much could be said here about the unique peculiarities of the French and their music. Just look at their organs! By this, of course, I mean the difference between German Baroque pipe organ and the French Baroque pipe organ. Different as night and day. The French prefer the subtle, nasal shimmerings of stringy and reedy sounds, while the Germans prefer the more bombastic, windy blasts of woody winds and brassy brass.

In essence, the French School can be summed up as follows:

1. From shoulder to knuckles is held rigid and still
2. The only movement is from the knuckles down
3. This enables you to play REALLY FAST
4. For volume, push HARDER

And that's it!

Years ago, I had the privilege of studying with a French master concert pianist of world renown. Though only 18 at the time, I had already been schooled in the *Anglo-Russian* tradition for 11 years. At the third lesson, the teacher in question stopped the lesson and gave this little speech: (I paraphrase, as time has eroded memory)

"You play ze peeano very well, Monsieur. You 'ave learned ze Russian English metode. I use zee French metod! To teach you, I would 'ave to undo all zat you 'ave learned and start from zee scratch, how you say? So why not we say goodbye now? You play your way and I'll play my way."

And although I had to pay him the full amount for that last lesson, although it was only really ½ a lesson with a dismissal, it was one of the MOST PLEASANT DIVORCES of my entire professional career and I shall always be grateful for his wisdom. I'd write him and thank him but, to quote Jacques Brel (who was a Belgian and NOT FRENCH), "...you see, I've forgotten his name."

The American School of Piano Playing
The American School, in summary:
1. The pianah is a PERCUSSIVE INSTRUMENT
2. As such, it *don't* matter how ya hit thuh keys
3. For louder, hit harder
4. There were Americans in the time of C.P.E. Bach, since he refers to the annoyance he felt when "thumpers" played the piano
5. Not *all* American pianists are thumpers – it depends on who they studied with
6. Never mind

Well, there you have it. Call me old-fashioned but that's what I believe and my ears and heart constantly confirm what I believe to be true. Check your teacher's credentials, look for pedigree if you can, but above all when you play the piano:
MAKE MUSIC, NOT MINCEMEAT
PLAY! DON'T TYPE
SING! DON'T BANG
And for God's sake
KNOW SOMETHING ABOUT HOW YOU'RE PLAYING.
You can KNOW all about a piece of music but not be able to

communicate that knowledge because you don't have the technique – you don't know how to press those keys down – to show that knowledge.

ALSO, on the other hand –

You may have the best "technique" in the world, but if you don't UNDERSTAND the music you're playing, all is lost.

It drives me to distraction when a student is playing *Minuet in B-flat*, clearly marked as such at the top of the page and you ask them what KEY the piece is in and they say"

"Gee, I dunno ...!"

You *must* know the key, the form, the period, the composer, the style, etc., etc., etc. before you start putting your pinkies down to "learn" the piece. Far more study should be done "off the page" than is currently in vogue. However, I'm getting on my pedagogical high horse and the smell of Lucetta's Turnip and Tripe Surprise is really getting to me, so I must investigate.

If I survive supper unscathed, I'll see you in the next chapter.

Chapter 15:
What Everyone Should Know About Blanche and Aloys

This is not an amusing chapter. There is not a single joke or one funny line. I'm sorry, but I might as well state this right off the top so's we know where we stand. So if it's innuendo or clever double entendre you're after, you might as well move onto the next chapter. Now, I haven't written it yet, but I'll need a laugh after I get through this one, so it should be good.

Second, I'm not going to tell you immediately who Blanche and Aloys are. I shall deal with the PROBLEM first and then introduce ALOYS, then BLANCHE. You shall have to speculate until the time of revelation ...

Possible Speculations re: Blanche and Aloys
- an early Vaudeville team
- the predecessors of Siegfried and Roy
- two old ushers at the Four Square Gospel Hall
- the two cows that replaced Lucy & Maude

FIRST, however, THE PROBLEM:

Many teachers of the piano, and even many Conservatories of Music, believe the following falsehood:

1. To play the piano, you need TECHNIQUE
2. Technique comes from practising SCALES, CHORDS & ARPEGGIOS
3. Then you can practise your pieces.

This could not be more WRONG.

As a matter of fact, it's about the WRONGEST thing you could say about technique and learning to play the piano.

So (you say) what's the truth? How does one learn to play the piano properly? What, then, is real "technique"?

Well let's look first at some

Hardcore Facts About the Fingers and Hands:

1. - fingers, thumbs, and Left and Right are not created EQUALLY
   - the thumb (or 1) is short, functions in opposition and slides laterally
   - 3 & 4 have junctures or tiny bridges between the tendons, making the independent movement of 4 (the ring finger) difficult
   - 3 is long and tends to bend inwardly at the last joint

- 5 (the "pinky") is the smallest of the fingers and weakest, largely due to its lack of use in so many basic functions
- 2 (the "index finger" or "pointer") is used so much it gets overburdened or stiff
- depending on whether you're right- or left-handed, the other one's weaker.

In short, of the team of 8 fingers and 2 thumbs that are used to play the piano, we have an UNEQUAL distribution of strength. And yet when playing the piano, we require equal strength and equal independence.

2. If you take these unequal, interdependent fingers and thumbs and practise scales, chords and arpeggios till the cows come home, you never clear up the inequalities or interdependencies. Yes, they all get stronger from pushing the keys up and down, but since scales, for example, require smooth EVEN playing, there is NOTHING in the practising of the scales that will fix up the natural, innate unevenness that exists among the fingers and thumbs. Therefore:

3. SPECIAL EXERCISES ARE REQUIRED

You must have special exercizes that will work SPECIFICALLY on ALL of the INEQUALITIES amongst the FINGERS and THUMBS to work toward making them INDEPENDENT AND EQUAL. Then, and only then, can you practise your scales, chords and arpeggios. You bring to them your now EQUAL and INDEPENDENT digits and learn them in half the time and play them twice as good (or well)

THE FORMULA FOR PROPER PRACTISING

FIRST: Technique
- special exercizes to correct the natural imbalances among your digits and create EQUALITY and INDEPENDENCE

SECOND: Scales, Chords & Arpeggios
- to develop a feel, dexterity and awareness of playing in the different keys as a preparation for playing pieces in a variety of keys up until the 20th century, when keys go berserk and it's God-help-you time anyway!

THIRD: Pieces
- the playing of actual music, which comes so much easier

and faster if step one is observed first. Do you see, Dear Pursuer of Pianistic Pleasures, THE IMPORTANCE OF TECHNIQUE?

How can I obtain technique?

Are there exercises that will correct the imbalances and give me 10 DIGITS that will function as:

1. a balanced squadron that will successfully attack the enemy (eg. a Beethoven sonata)

2. a well-rounded complementary team that will carry the ball (eg. a Brahms intermezzo) to victory (ie. 1st prize in the Chezlee Festival)

3. a tightly knit management team of experts with no loose cannons that with their presentation (eg. Debussy's *Golliwog's Cake Walk*) will bring their company profits (ie. standing ovations and the Maestro Colli Albani Scholarship and free bottle of booze)?

The answer is YES!

And, in case you've forgotten the question, (as I had) I'll be repetitious just this once: THERE IS A GROUP OF EXERCISES THAT WILL HELP YOU! MAY I INTRODUCE YOU TO:

Aloys Schmitt!

Aloys Schmitt (1788-1866) was a German pianist and eminent teacher. The son and pupil of a cantor, he composed a number of works but alas, today he is known, virtually solely, for a book of exercises for the piano.

Officially, it is entitled: *SCHMITT: FIVE FINGER EXERCISES* Op.16 (and the best edition is one by the famous Canadian composer Healey Willan, published by Frederick Harris and with some of Willan's own exercises at the end, which are terrific).

Once you crack the cover, you find the following description and I quote it in full. The words in big type are MY editorial comments of importance and significance:

"PREPARATORY EXERCISES to obtain INDEPENDENCE and EQUALITY in the actions of the fingers. Each exercise should be played at least 15 times; omitting the crotchet at the end until the last repetition. The exercises should be played first with the *right hand alone,* then with the *left hand alone*; and lastly with both hands together *WITHOUT THE*

THE THING I'VE PLAYED WITH THE MOST

LEAST MOTION OF THE HANDS. They should at first be played VERY SLOWLY increasing rapidily as the fingers gather strength and freedom."

Now, just a little sidebar here and that is that I'm dropping pearls of wisdom here and revealing secrets that have been handed down for generations since Beethoven and before and for which my parents forked over a fortune for me to take the lessons. Now, you're paying less than $20.00. for this book and to my mind that's pretty cheap for "pearls," so you should be grateful. Now, back to Schmitt:

And here's where we also tie into my great-grand-teacher Tobias Matthay when we explain the phrase WITHOUT THE LEAST MOTION IN THE HANDS.

Remember the F.A.R.K. principle from the previous chapter? (Go look it up if you have to.)

F.A.R.K. = *F* ingers
          A lways
          R esting *on* the
          K eys

The fingers must ALWAYS rest ON the keys and never lose contact with them. Here's the proper position:

ARMS	parallel to the keyboard
KNUCKLES	arched as if holding an orange
WRIST	not raised and relaxed
FINGER PADS &	
SIDE OF THE THUMBS	resting ON the Keys always

From this relaxed position
1. The Finger Pushes the Key *Down*
2. The Finger RELAXES
3. The *KEY* PUSHES the FINGER *UP*

VOLUME IS NOT IMPORTANT IN DEPRESSING THE KEY! BEING RELAXED is IMPORTANT and letting the action of the key push the finger up, without ever taking the finger OFF the KEY.

Further points to remember when practising your Schmitt:
1. Practise SLOWLY, focusing on HOW you're depressing the key, not HOW FAST.
2. Practise hands separately for ages until you're really getting the FEEL OF THE KEYS whereby your fingers

and the keys ARE ONE. Sounds sort of Zen-like, but after a while, it becomes true.

3. When you get to holding notes down, press these notes down FIRST, then start the exercizes.

4. Things to Watch Out For that INDICATE YOU'RE NOT RELAXED AND LETTING JUST THE FINGERS DO THE WORK:

a) other fingers flying OFF the keys as you depress a key.

b) Other fingers pushing keys down a bit when the one playing finger is working.

To sum up: "FLY OFFS" and "PRESS DOWNS" means lack of strength, relaxation, etc. So slow down, relax, FOCUS..

5. 15 times is not as important as a couple of times done properly. It's better to do an exercise ONCE in the proper way than 100 times unfocused and improperly.

6. Crotchet is the English word for quarter note and you can simply ignore it.

7. Every so often, just take your HAND off the keys, shake it out, relax, take a breath then recommence. Intense focusing can create tension, which becomes counter-productive to relaxation.

8. The finger/thumb must always be completely relaxed, exposed to its "weakest" and not using any effort from hand, wrist, arm, etc. in depressing the key. It's only as you expose your finger alone to its weakest, most re laxed, vulnerable state that you can begin to develop strength.

9. Any other questions, write me c/o Mrs. Biggar's Budgie and Lube Shop, Main St. Chezlee Ont, attn post-mistress Queenie McQuaigue (she's a dear friend and always makes sure I get it).

Now, as this is a humorous volume, I'm going to stop here because I'm almost on the verge of becoming too serious.

However, I do hear your cry coming through loud and clear and that is: "Who the *hell* is BLANCHE, then?"

DANGER! PROCEED WITH CAUTION! YOU MUST BE OF AN AGE TO CONTINUE!! FATAL CONSEQUENCES COULD RESULT!

A few years back, as I lay in the Intensive Care Unit of the Chezlee Ont General Marine and Cattle Hospital, hooked up to a pile of machines as they attempted to discover the possible path of a suspected blood clot that could, when projected, proceed to my brain, I despaired of my life and regretted terribly that I had so much still to do.

Modern medical practice hummed and hawed and finally sent me back to Obscuria to "rest quietly in the dark" and "don't move" and "contact your local doctor." I obeyed for a day and a half and then said "Phooey" and got up and sought the advice of Dr. Peter Blurgell, our local vet. He felt the place in the vein in my arm near the wrist where the suspected blood clot was and said:

"Have you had surgery recently?"

"Yes," I said, "I had a sub-mucal resection a few months past."

"Did they have trouble hooking you up to the IV?" our local vet questioned further.

"Ah ... let me think... why, yes, yes they did. They had a lot of trouble. Shoved that needle in several times, they did," I recalled in horror.

"That's it, then!" he said.

"What's it, then?" I replied

"Your blood clot, you great ninny" he joked. "It's not a blood clot at all. It's SCAR TISSUE from a BUNGLED IV." And he started to put his equipment away.

"And what about the tingling sensation from above the elbow to the wrist in that arm?" I queried, demandingly.

"Have you been doing any strenuous or strange exercizes with your arms lately?" He flashed back, seeming to begin to lose patience with me.

"Please, Peter, I'm a musician" I said. "I take great care of my fingers, hands and arms, why I even ..."

Suddenly it hit me!

"Wait a minute! I've been doing Blanche for the last three weeks! Could it be her?" I asked quizzically.

When I showed him the sorts of things I'd been doing with my Blanche, he said:

"No wonder! You've pinched a nerve in your elbow. That's the tingles. The clot is just scar tissue! You're healthy as a horse, Anthon."

I tell you, I fair skipped out of Peter's and down to the Ox & Udder to have a Ripple or three to make up for the angst and trauma of the days preceding.

"So who the Hell is Blanche and what the Hell did she do to you?" I can already hear echoing through the annals of time, so may I introduce to you (drum roll please):

MISS BLANCHE RENNIE (Ta-dah!)

If you look her up in Baker's *Biographical Dictionary of Music and Musicians*, you will not find her. And to the best of my knowledge, the only publication I'm aware of is a collection of exercizes, printed in 1925 and called *HAND CULTURE*.

HAND CULTURE
for
PIANISTS, VIOLINISTS AND CELLISTS
FINGER, HAND AND ARM GYMNASTICS
AT THE PIANO
giving
STRENGTH, FREEDOM AND
INDEPENDENCE
by
BLANCHE H. RENNIE
TEACHER OF PIANO AT THE BIRMINGHAM SCHOOL OF MUSIC

HAND CULTURE for

a) Strengthening and rendering supple fingers, hands and arms.

b) Giving freedom (lateral and vertical) and absolute in dependence to each finger

c) Lateral movement of fingers and hands

d) Rotary exertions (and non-exertions)

e) Rotary movement of forearm

f) Rotary movement of upper arm

g) Freedom in passing the thumb under the hand and hand over the thumb for scale and arpeggio playing

h) Loosening knuckles wrists, elbows, and shoulders

i) Strengthening the muscles of the shoulder, back and side ** The exercises of Group IV, especially 5-10 and 13-18, are invaluable for this purpose, as well as loosening the shoulders, elbows and wrists

** These muscles, which have to bear the weight of the arms and take all the strain which playing involves, are, as a rule, entirely neglected, while really they need very special help, and students and artists will be amply repaid for the little time spend on these exercises by the attainment of greater freedom and ease, greater power and greater endurance.

The book is replete with nice oval pictures of old Blanche as she demonstrates how to do her exercises.

The stretching and strengthening that Blanche puts your through is INCREDIBLE. Once you've learned all the exercises and start going through them on a daily basis for a month or so, you feel as if you could rip the New York phone book in half easily with your fingers alone.

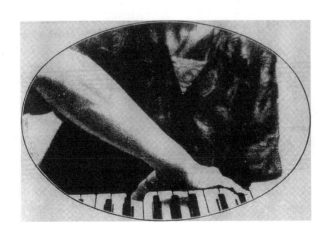

But, there are some cautionary guides.

WORDS OF WARNING BEFORE GETTING INTO BLANCHE:

1. Tackle Blanche only when puberty is thoroughly finished and you're essentially dealing with the grown hand.

2. Tackle Blanche only when at an advanced level of piano playing.

3. Tackle Blanche only when you have thoroughly mastered your SCHMITT (including the Willan exercises).

4. Read EVERYTHING Blanche tells you to do and do *only* and *exactly* what she says.

5. Always, constantly, RELAX and take frequent breaks and shake out your fingers and hands so you don't GET TOO TENSE, PINCH A NERVE and END UP IN HOSPITAL WITH A BLOOD CLOT! (see above).

6. Don't take BLANCHE as a regular part of your piano diet but only as a "de temps en temps" retreat for strengthening and toning up.

7. Do not OVERDO BLANCHE! Remember what happened to Robert Schumann!!!!

And, you know, I'm going to leave Blanche there, if you don't mind. Serious students can give me a call and we could set up lessons (My rates are cheap but I need the income as I'm making *nada* from printing books.)

Dear General Reader, it's enough to know (and joyously, too) that Scales, Chords and Arpeggios are secondary. But Aloys (and Blanche – later) are a MUST. And Bob's your uncle (although in my case it's Roy).

Chapter 16:
The Chamber of Horrors – The Piano Student Recital

1976 was, to quote a phrase used by our current reigning monarch, an ANNUS HORRIBILUS. Aphids infested the asparagus patch, Lucetta's rutabaga chips went rancid in June, the Maestro got ptomaine poisoning and wandered off for seven weeks and it was the worst Student Piano Recital of my entire career.

I shall never forget that evening. I'd rented the Four Square Gospel Hall and it was packed with friends and family, ex's and offspring, hopefuls and no-way-José's.

Rhythmless Raymond was the first one up. Mind you, I never called him Rythmless Raymond, though that indeed was the state he was in. He had ABSOLUTELY NO concept of time, beat, pulse, rhythm whatsoever. I had tried everything to get him to play in time. Metronomes, drums, guns ... but alas, to no avail. It drove me nuts as week after week he would kill another sonatina or berceuse, lost in a rhythmless mush of notes that gave you no idea what piece he was playing. Finally I had said to him,

"Is there a pop piece you'd like to murde ...er...ah... I mean ... play?"

Well, after some thought he said he wanted to work on *The Piano Roll Blues*. And so we did.

Six months later, it was no better than when we'd started and the student recital proved no exception.

Rhythmless Raymond stumbled through *The Piano Roll Blues* without playing a single bar in the correct time. As he wallowed and splayed through 4½/4 slash 6¼/8 time signatures, the audience started to tap their feet or tap their hands on their knees to try and help Rhythmless Raymond GET THE BEAT. The movement throughout the house in the audience's vain attempt to help him, grew to such a frenzy that Rows 3, 9 and 17 completely tipped over backwards, tossing the inhabitants of the seats in Rows 3, 9 and 17 to fall into the laps of persons sitting in Rows 4, 10 and 18. The commotion was such that Raymond mistook it for a sudden outburst of praise and ovation, so he stopped playing (he was near the end I think, anyways) and took a long bow while the ushers tried to re-structure the Gospel Hall seating.

Prynthia Thalmus was one of my best students and she was next up to play. I had always enjoyed Prynthia's lessons, as she worked hard and played with exquisite musical taste. She was to play the well-known Chopin *E-flat Nocturne*. And she would have done it beautifully.

Beautifully, that is, if the little accident hadn't happened. That afternoon, at volleyball practice, Prynthia had done something to the fourth finger of her right hand. They had obviously not been able to contact anyone from the medical profession but had instead procured the services of someone from public works. She had a "drain-pipe" on her tiny third finger, right hand, that augmented its size to gargantuan proportions. Her mother, Mrs. P. Thalmus, was a very tight-lipped, pharisaical sort of woman of a parsimonious nature who confronted me before the recital and said:

"Prynthia's been playing this piece for six months so she's damn well going to play it!"

Starting with the second note of that formerly exquisitely beautiful melody of the *E-flat Nocturne*, the poor, damaged Prynthian hand clunked down a cluster of notes when one alone should have rung out clear and sweet.

Instead of 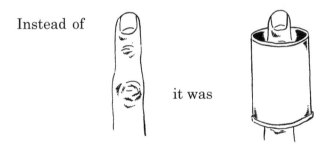 it was

due to the drain-pipe-like device on her R.H.3.

The sounds were painful. Children squirmed, a Dalmatian in the back row started yelping and crying and three dogs parked outside on leashes began a chorus of howls, reminiscent of the Baskervilles. Some audience members openly plugged their ears and for some reason, the dissonances seemed to affect the kidney area, as there were several over-hasty retreats to the washrooms by both sexes. So between the howling and baying, and to-ing and fro-ing, it became hard to hear poor Prynthia's ill-treated *Nocturne*. Finally, it was Mrs. Thalmus who shouted out, "Oh, for God's sake, Prithee, stop it!" And she did and we were all so very grateful.

Laetitia (the 'e' is unpronounced) was next on the roster. Laetitia was one of my adult students and I've always loved and admired my adult students. To make and take the time in the busy stress of an adult life to study the piano is an admirable quality and Laetitia had been doing it for years. I was not her first teacher, however. No, she had studied with 20 other teachers, all now deceased.

Her last instructress, prior to Laetitia's coming to study with me, had in her dying breath whispered faintly to Laetitia,

"If you forget ...(cough, cough, choke choke)..., always go back to the beginning."

Now, whether this deathbed advice was general and applied to life as a whole, or specific and applied to public recitals of a Mozart sonata when there are memory slips, is uncertain. Laetitia, however, took an exclusively pianistic interpretation of the penultimate epithet of her dying tutor, and, if she ever had a memory slip in a bagatelle or rondo, she would immediately RETURN TO THE BEGINNING.

Laetitia had made not insignificant progress in her pianoforte studies and had advanced, tenuously albeit, to working on some of the easier Mozart sonatas. We had spent 17 months on the overly well-known K. 545 in C major first movement and she knew it backwards and forwards. "Nerves" however had been a chronic problem with dear Miss Lippe (the 'e' is unpronounced) and they affected her most under the pressure of any kind of public performance. I always remember once at a Kiwanis Club banquet thanking all the volunteers who had worked so hard in eliminating a horrid blight that had attacked all the root vegetables, they had asked Miss Lippe (the 'e' unpronounced) to say a blessing before the meal. She had commenced with "Father, we thank you ..." and never got further. The deathbed dictum forced her to repeat it like a mantra until Bert Walch shouted out "My kidney's getting cold. AMEN!" Laetitia burst into tears and fled behind a potted palm and remained there until after the cream puffs and coffee were served.

My nerves were shredded the night of the student recital as she tiptoed her way up and across to the grand in a flowing gown of floral muslin and a silk shawl with fringe (not the sort of thing you'd wear for Mozart, I thought, but never mind.)

"*Dah-dah-dah-dee-diddle-dum*" – (I'm sure you recognize it as the beginning of the Mozart *C-major Piano Sonata K* – same number as on the last page) – began Laetitia and the entire audience were sitting on the edges of their seats, for her reputation had spread far and wide (as had also, her seat. Age had settled in her posterior, as it were, and she amply covered the bench, although ankles and wrists were almost delicately slim.)

"*Tah-tuca-tuca-tuca-tuca-tuca-tuca-tuca-tah,*" she was continuing on, and so far there was no problem. It was somewhere in her fourth series of "*Tah-tuca*'s" that I began to fret. It was a slight thing – a momentary tremor – but I knew her "nerves" had taken over and we were headed for disaster. She continued doing "*Tah-tuca*" sequences, however, trying to keep her aplomb.

As she was about to start her 19th "*Tah-tuca*" and was by this time well into the bass register, way down near the bottom of the keyboard, and getting very muddy, she knew she had to do something. Brilliantly, she began a chromatic scale in the R.H. that ascended from the underworld gutter she'd dug herself into and, once back into the normal register, cleverly landed on a C and began the opening bars of *Dah-dah-dah*, etc. FROM THE BEGINNING!

There was a look of victorious pride on the Lippe ('e' unpronounced) face as she began AGAIN FROM THE BEGINNING and you could almost hear her saying "See, Miss Mangley, I remembered what you said."

As she proceeded and came quickly to the "*Tah-tuca*" section, she made a decision. "Last time, I went down and got completely lost. This time I'll ascend and see if that works out any better."

Needless to say, it didn't. As she was about to go off the keyboard (her "*tuca*'s" had gone so high this time) she suddenly made a dramatic pause – sniffled boldly – and started from the beginning BUT IN THE MINOR KEY. By this time, Mozart was turning in his grave, I was churning in my seat, and Flo Legge was taking bets at the back as to whether Laetitia would make it or not.

Ultimately during the next 11 minutes, which seemed more like 2 weeks, Miss Lippe ('e' unpronounced) never got beyond bar 7½ and during that time THE BEGINNING was played a total of 41 times with little variation.

Her final solution of a cadence to get the agony over and end the damn thing by using the last line of *O, Canada* in the key of A major was actually a stroke of genius. The audience had been writhing in agony throughout the repetitious torture and resembled:

a) an early Flemish painting of Hell

b) anything by Salvador Dali

c) a boneless chicken ranch.

With the advent of the national anthem, the entire audience – men and women, children and the Dalmatian at the back of the church – rose to its feet, sang the last phrase, "...stand on guard for thee," and burst into thunderous applause, yells and whistles of delight and relief and several of the men shouted "Play ball!" – forgetting where they were.

There is an inverse relationship between agony and ecstasy: The deeper and longer the agony, the more ecstatic the ecstasy when the agony is finally over. Bland usually follows bland, but Hell on a grand scale is followed by a tumultuous burst of praise when it's finally over that falsely represents the aesthetic worth of the event.

Miss Lippe (still with the 'e' unpronounced) modestly took several curtsies to the cheering throng and even had a smug smile on her face. The credit for that I give to the late Miss Mangley, no questions asked.

Verna Quansit was next in line and Laetitia's bung-up, ended up being a hard act to follow. Verna was one of my brightest, most intellectual students. Her cranial skills, however, were largely in the mathematical slash scientific vein and the skills on that side left her aesthetically depleted. As a matter of fact, she was completely tone deaf. She couldn't tell the difference between an unaccompanied violin sonata of Bach and rain falling on the corrugated tin roof on the barn slash garage on Obscuria's back 50. God had obviously replaced her ear drum with some leather-like substance at birth and Verna had lived since then in a non-tonal world.

Now, as long as she had the correct music in front of her,

Verna was fine. Her scientific brain directed her to do everything correctly and that she would. It was not the most "musical" playing one had ever heard, but she played the piece absolutely correctly and even slowed down or sped up where I'd marked it in the score. Because she only played by following, robot-like, every note I'd made in the score, I had dropped the Clara Schumann dictum that performers MUSTN'T USE MUSIC and said that Verna could. And as long as Verna had the score with her, she played quite acceptably.

We had ventured into the popular genre for a bit during her early teen years and had worked up a goodly version of Scott Joplin's *Maple Leaf Rag* which she was playing quite properly.

The afternoon of that student recital, Verna's younger sister, Vilene, had learned to draw sharps in her Grade III music class and had come home and drawn them all over Verna's copy of Scott Joplin's *Maple Leaf Rag*.

The night of the concert, confident Verna boldly marched to the piano, plunked down the now disfigured score, and played exactly what was written, totally oblivious to the aural affects that the last minute additional sharps would have had.

AN AVERAGE AUDIENCE MEMBER
LISTENING TO VERNA QUANSITE'S
MAPLE LEAF RAG.

The smug smirk of self-satisfaction permeated through the mangled *Rag*. She did not see the sudden shudders, the eye-scrunching looks of pain, the total body spasms and the utter agonized angst of every single musical member of that audience. Even the Dalmatian started yelping and piddled on Wilda Wamborough's bumbershoot lying on the floor. Only the superior, confident look on Verna's face prevented me or any audience member from shouting "Stop the insanity!" The fact that she was totally oblivious to the horrendous dissonances that were pouring out of that piano's sounding board became the focus of everyone's attention. In spite of the pain, we all were riveted, stunned and stupefied by the fact that she carried on NOTWITHSTANDING.

When she plunked down the last chord – which, with the addition of Vilene's sharps bore no resemblance to any sounds heard within our planetary system – the audience jumped to its feet as one body, expressing gratitude that the insanity had stopped, and making comments like:

a) "Unbelievable …simply unbelievable!"

b) "I've never heard the like …"

c) "If I hadn't heard it with my own ears, I never would have believed it."

Fortunately for the music community in Chezlee Ont, Verna got pregnant shortly after the recital and moved down the township line to the hamlet of Spry, where she co-habited with a chinchilla farmer and hasn't been seen or heard of since.

Harlem Trotter was the last boy up. His parents had named him Harlem (although their last name was Trotter) because his paternal grandfather's name was Harry and his maternal grandfather's name was Clem. Harlem, they felt, combined the two beautifully and made both grandsires happy. The fact that Harlem Trotter was not black, nor a basketball player, never bothered the Trotters, probably through ignorance more than anything else, otherwise they would have given him the middle name of Globe. The fact that his middle name was Lezlee confirmed the parental ignorance, although I still think he'd have a rough time if he moved to New Jersey.

Harlem was a solid player who was advancing well and practised his instrument diligently. We'd chosen for his recital piece the lovely *Romance* by Sibelius in *D-flat major* with that lovely scale run starting in the bass, running up to the middle, then splitting with each hand going in opposite directions to the climax of the crashing chords that bring the piece to its glorious and stirring finale.

Harlem had practised the piano studiously and had worked extra hard on that cadenzal scale run that was technically challenging and also the kind of fanfare flourish that leads us into the grand finale of the whole piece. He had played it correctly only a few times before the recital and I had warned him that if he didn't have a decent number of "correct times" under his belt, the pressures of public performance could bring out one of the bunged-up versions if he didn't get some more correct ones into his head and fingers. He'd worked his little fingers to the bone in the days and nights preceding the concert and, at the rehearsal at Obscuria before the recital, had played the entire piece beautifully, especially the scale run.

That night of the student recital, Harlem walked to the grand with a poise and maturity admirable for his mid-adolescent years. He sat down confidently and the audience breathed a sigh of relief. They had been through Hell up to this point in the evening but they felt that at last their trials were ended, their sufferings over, and they could sit back, relax and ENJOY for the first time that evening.

And they did! Up to a point! The Sibelius had been going swimmingly. Impeccable accuracy, with deeply sensitive expressiveness uncharacteristic of a teenage boy of Harlem's masculinity, had combined to lull the audience into the raptures of aural delight. As Harlem approached the mighty scale cadenza leading up to the final chordal climax, a slight twitch of the memory of the difficulties he'd had flickered across my brow, but his performance thus far was so assured and strong, I dismissed the fleeting doubt and settled down to simply revel.

The scale ascended from the depths and split in the middle. Halfway through the cascading, catapulting figures as the R.H. sought the very upper extremities of the keyboard and the L.H. was plunging to the lowest bass notes, he goofed. The fingers fumbled. Knotted tone clusters replaced glittering scale runs. The cadenza was wrecked. Harlem plucked his fingers from the keys and in the shocked silence (for the entire audience had been shocked out of their reverie of aural delights) Harlem in a clear, loud and unmistakably distinct voice, said:
    "F..ck!"

It was, how shall I say it, matter of fact. Disappointed, rather than angered. Frustrated but not unreasonable. It was more as if he was really saying:

"Well, gosh darn it all. I really practised that bit a lot and I have played it correctly many times. What a goldarn pity I've screwed it up. Oh well, here it goes again."

He recommenced the passage, and to be perfectly honest with you, dear reader, I, and no member of the audience, knew if he got it right the second time or not. Everything was put into a state of suspended animation after that single expeletive. It was as if the piece went on to the finish, he bowed, we clapped. The recital ended. We had tea and tarts and rutabaga chips. But it was all like a silent film. The only sound heard was the universal reverberations of that one four-letter word echoing through our incredulous minds. The only real dialogue that ensued after Harlem's four-letter expression of his frustration were phrases like:

a) "Did he really say that?"

b) "It must have been something else!"

c) "God'll get you for that!" (that was the Trotters, as they were Fellowship Baptist and strict).

d) "Surely I made the whole thing up and it never really happened".

To this day, no one has, to my knowledge, ever publicly acknowledged that they heard it. It's a bit like at old man Stubble's funeral, when Lucetta had been having trouble digesting grains and, right at the point when Rev. McDudd said "Ashes to ashes, dust to dust," had let rip with the largest, loudest windbreaker I've ever heard in my life. Its orchestral dimensions were so phenomenal that no one then or since ever acknowledged that it occurred.

Funny, that, isn't it? Some of life's best jokes remain undiscussable.

Anyway, attending student piano recitals is about as much fun as going to a public hanging, so I hope you haven't had to go to too many.

I myself don't hold them anymore. And so far, nobody's objected.

A Divertimento:
Alternative Styles from Rags to Rock!

When it comes to alternatives, the Maestro and I have no problem whatsoever in dealing openly and honestly with them, as we have been called "alternatively styled" for years by some of the more staid and locked-in-the-past members of our community. Presbyterian groups particularly have perpetrated Calvinistic judgements no only on our music but on our unique domestic arrangement, and "alternative" is actually one of the nicer terms they've used. So while we are staunch supporters of and participants in the CLASSICAL brand of music, we have no problem whatsoever in climbing out on some of these stranger limbs of the tree of music and talking quite openly and freely about the odder twigs and leaves of the piano tree.

And honestly, dear reader, there is such a plethora of different pianistic styles that have developed over the years, it is ONCE AGAIN impossible to be comprehensive and include everybody. So what I'm proposing to do is to take you on a
ROMP AROUND CHEZLEE ONT
and visit some of the dives, bistri and hangouts of our little rural community and, from the particular, give you a view of some of the "other" ways of playing the piano.

Francine Moletard at the B.M.E.

Chezlee Ont has always been extremely proud of its not-inconsiderably-sized black community. When slaves managed to get on the famous Underground Railroad, many stayed on right to the end, which happened to be right here, or rather, near here. The end of the line was actually in Crudsville, which is about "25 mile down the road" but, the African-Americans quickly established a thriving community here that's over 100 years old.

Francine Moletard is the pianist for the British Methodist and Episcopal Church, also known as the "colored" church, and has been so since her youth. Natural talent, years of practice and work with touring groups that would come to the B.M.E for

special "musical" missions made Francine one of the top rag/
boogie/blues/gospel (black) pianists within miles. She exercised
NO discrimination when it came to playing for the church. She
would accompany the finest Anglican hymn to a tune like
Ebenezer and make the Archbishop of Canterbury happy. She
could then do an offertory of *Look to the Hills* in the best combination of rag/boogie I'd ever heard. And her blues/ gospel (black)
playing was unbeatable.

Lucetta and I used to try to slip into the back row of the
B.M.E. on a warm summer's eve and listen and marvel as
Francine tickled those ivories. Not that we couldn't have sat
front and centre, as they were always accepting, warmly wel-
coming and thrilled to see us. We just preferred the back row in
case Lucetta took one of her turns.

To this day, and largely due to Francine, I love to listen to
rags and boogie-woogie, while my appreciation for the blues slash
gospel (black) tradition simply grows and grows.

These are styles that are learned only by observation, imi-
tation and development. I remember trying to get the Bumsteed
boy to play boogie-woogie. He could get neither the boogie nor
the woogie and my frustration boiled over one day at his acute
aural thickness and I hit him over the head with the second
volume of the Schnabel edition of the Beethoven sonatas. The
Beethoven had quite an affect on him in the nature of a severe
cranial bump. Needless to say, old man Burnsteed came round
and beat the living daylights out of me the next night, but at
least the boy stopped coming, gratefully ending my boogie-woogie
nightmare!

The point to be made here, I think, if indeed there is one, is
that as much as one can diet on Bach to Bartok, it's nice to occasionally munch on a Scott Joplin rag or some real good black
gospel piano playing. I tell you, there's nothing better to put a
little oomph into a sagging second movement or a bogged-down
bagatelle.

Jade Jones the Jazz Guy

Jade was a unique member of our little community. He never
married. Never talked much. Wasn't from here. Played by ear.
But every Saturday afternoon at the Ox & Udder, Jade would
improvise on old jazz standards in such a unique way that his
fame spread from Bessborough to Miller's Lake. He smoked tons

of cigarettes. He never smiled. And nobody really knew anything about him.

Now, jazz piano, and the field of jazz in general, is tingled with a certain melancholic hue. As fast and sassy as a jazz piece can get, there is still a kind of tragic beauty at its heart. Jazz is best listened to after ordering several stiff ones.

Cigarettes are essential and the quiet, perhaps self-pitying reflection that occurs while listening to it is enough to force even the strongest and most stable among us on to Prozac.

Jade Jones was a MASTER at using his gifted fingers to tug on the nostalgic heartstrings of his listeners. Single older ones listened and wished they had. Separated and divorced devotées listened and wished they hadn't. Either way, that Ox & Udder was crowded every Saturday afternoon and the gin flowed like the ballpark toilet when it breaks down every Spring.

There are tons of jazz greats but I feel Jade is one of the unsung masters of the genre. Just because you know and love Hummel and Franck doesn't mean you don't cry into a Black Russian over *Green Mountain Home* or *Misty*.

The Peckernaught Boys

The Peckernaught boys formed their own rock and roll group. They all had studied with me and once they knew three chords they left, as it was "too much" for them! Now, I know there are a few rock and roll greats, but the Peckernaughts were not among them. And as the synthesizer has replaced the acoustic piano in most of the rock groups we know of round here, there's not much I can teach the little buggers once they've learned their three chords.

I must confess a little prejudice here due to my own personal history. When rock and roll was born with such delightful hits as *Rock Around the Clock* and *Jailhouse Rock*, I was already flattening my dominant 13th chords and doing 4th and 5th species counterpoint, though I was barely into my teens. Three-chord, root-position songs did not overly thrill me, even if they all were 7ths. Granted, rock and roll did ascend to the brilliant heights of the Beatles and Elton John can play the piano after a fashion and they're all much richer than either the Maestro or I ever will be, but I did and do find some of it banal and boring.

Although I will and do expose myself to it, I find I can't stand being long exposed and quickly wrap my raincoat back around me after just a little bit of exposure.

I've even gone to a dance at the Agriculture Fair that featured the Peckernaught boys and actually tapped my foot to the music during one of their numbers. However, it's not my favorite art form and I'm just going to leave it at that. I'm not going to apologize or justify it, I'm just stating it and leaving it.

Velma Spragge and Marvell Pye

Velma Spragge and Marvell Pye have played the two grands (both donated) at the Central Missionary and Nazarene Assembly for 35 years. They have also lived together for the same period of time and although Marvel tends to wear suits, cowboy boots, neckties, and cropped crew cuts, while Velma sports chiffon, gold-dyed waves and overworked cosmetics, no one ever raises queries about them and I am certainly not going to be the one to start.

As it is a Fundamentalist milieu in which Velma & Marvell

operate, their musical style I would typify as white gospel. Its origins are not African and black "soul" music, but stem more from the worst of the Victorian era from General William Booth's rousing ditties for the Sally Ann to Louis Gottschalk's melodramatic slop. (Did you know Gottschalk hated the Irish openly and deplored Christianity in almost all its forms?)

Velma and Marvell were good at their white gospel, but it's a style that's dying out and there's certainly no one to replace them at Central. And I know, if either of them "goes," they're going to phone me and I know I can't and don't want to but they're going to be offended but I can't help it, so I hope and earnestly wish that Velma and Marvell outlive the possibility of my usefulness.

Darla Draine

Darla Draine was and is a flower-child hippie. She still wears floor-length diaphonous formless dresses that are Javex-dyed and no shoes. She has never used traditional medicine in her life and there are some parts of her anatomy which could use some. She writes her own songs and accompanies herself on the pianoforte. She suffers from acute arpeggio-itus in her accompaniments and her texts are rarely decipherable and range between only two poles, namely 1) angry protests against just about everything and 2) bland, nebulous sweet songs about absolutely nothing but people go "oooh" and "aaaah" and think she is great. Folk music is an age-old genre but once each generation has found its folk-niche it tends to be a dead-end street or a cul-de-sac out of which one cannot get. Darla certainly reached her artistic apex about three decades ago and is merely tolerated as a kind of local phenomenon, similar to Itchey Bill, the town drunk, and Old Man Dowker, who distributes Gospel tracks.

Folk music is simple but there's only so simple you can get before you become banal. Darla has been beyond banal for years, but she's a nice person so we all try to show an interest – although improvement in her personal hygiene would enhance our ability to sit through one of her songs.

I hope that this highly specific personal romp through Chezlee has made you aware of other pianistic traditions and will broaden your awareness of alternatives!

Appendix A: Terms

Accordion: Formerly (ca. 1100 BC) called the SHENG, it is associated with *Lady of Spain* and tawdry evenings on the Champs Elysées. It's trying to turn into a legitimate Olympic-recognized instrument and is generally succeeding. The FREE BASS form of accordion has been attacked by Ian Paisly and 17 of the Baptist denominations as being antithetical to the 10 Commandments and the Baltimore catechism.

Bebung: A vibrato effect peculiar to the clavichord. Once the finger pushes the key down, the finger does a repeated pressure motion that increases the tension of the string and leads to a slight variation in pitch. You MUST NOT "over bebung," as it can produce that too-wide wobble of an aging church soloist whereby the central pitch of the note is completely unfathomable due to the wide course of its alteration. BUT, under the right circumstances, bebunging can be a delightful experience – and I mean that in both ways: either bebunging yourself or having bebunging done for you.

C.B.S.: Bought our Steinway in 1972.

Cimbalon: See Dulcimer, see Psaltery, see your doctor.

Clavicembalo: See Harpsichord (and when you get there, see clavicembalo).

Clavichord: Developed in the 12th century from the monochord (see Monochord – feel free cause it's not contagious), an oblong wooden box (sort of like a small coffin) with legs or not. The strings are put into vibration by small brass wedges called tangents. (Not the kind that I'm accused of going on, or the ones the Maestro does go on.) It's a soft, delicate sound and you have to just about be resting your head on the ample bosom of the clavichordinettist to be able to hear the damn thing. You can, however, get some DYNAMIC levels as in BEBUNG-ing it. However, I would strongly advise that you look up BEBUNG-ing in this chapter on Terms before you try it yourself unguided. If you get Bebunged up, it can be painful and take some time to work out.

Clavicytherium: A harpsichord with a vertical body – 16th 17th century. Died out probably due to Anabaptist diatribes against vertical sex as it may lead to dancing. It is also difficult to pronounce, or get in through the front door.

Dulcimer: Same as Psaltery but strings were played by small hammers held in the hand. Goes back to ancient Assyria and Persia. There's a stone-carved picture found in Nineveh in 667 BCE of a man playing one.

Harpsichord: Sir Thomas Beecham described its sound as "Two skeletons copulating on a galvanized-tin roof." He also told a pianist he was trying to accompany, who was taking a lot of liberty with the rhythm, "What you need to accompany you, Madam, is not a symphony orchestra but an elastic band!" In spite of his sense of humor, he was a pretty good musician and he was related to the cough-drop lozenge Beecham's and somehow I forgot what term I was explaining, but it doesn't matter. I've had fun! Have you?

Klavier: German for piano, and depending on the century, it could mean any of the major keyboard instruments. A broad, general word (surprising for such a meticulous nation).

Lola Montez: one of the 26 love affairs enjoyed by the Abbot Liszt, who was no Father but did father many.

Monochord: A single string stretched over a wooden resonator with a movable fret attached so that the length (and therefore the pitch) can be varied. Invented by Pythagorus in the 6th century BCE. In later Middle Ages, number of strings increased to two or three. Overall, in my personal opinion, it must have been a bloody BORING instrument and not the sort of thing you'd want to hear at a hot party.

Psaltery: An ancient and Medieval instrument consisting of a flat sounding board over which a number of strings are stretched and plucked by the fingers. A PSALTERION is often mentioned in Greek literature. St. Jerome (330-420) used a 10- string psaltery shaped in a rectangle. The four sides were the four gospels and the 10 strings were the 10 Commandments. God knows where the 12 apostles were, but in 1620 Praetorius mentions a psaltery shaped liked a pig's head called the ISTROMENTO DI PORCO. Now, I've seen some porky instrumentalists but never a porcine instrument – although the double bass could qualify.

Silbermann, Gottfried (see Stein): worked for Frederick the Great, building pianofortes.

Stein: Johann Andreas Stein was an early piano maker trained by Silbermann. Also something to drink German beer out of.

Steinway: English for Steinweg.

Steinweg: German for Steinway

Van Cliburn: His real first names are Harvey Lavan and his father was an oil tycoon. He never married and still lives with his mother. He retired at 44 and contributed $50,000 to the 1985 Van Cliburn International Piano Competition. Honestly now, I ask you ...

Virginal: Is simply a 16th-century version of a harpsichord, described as early as 1511. Pedantic scholars beware! because there is no historical proof as to why they were called viginals, and any postulation that only virgins played them and then, when they lost their virginity, found something better to play with, is purely speculative. The *Fitzwilliam Virginal Book* contains 297 compositions by such great virginalists as Byrd, Morley, Philips, Farnaby, Bull, Weelkes, Tomkins and Gibbons – most of whom had kids so they were by no means virgins. Queen Elizabeth I was said to be virginalist and she never did marry so maybe that's how the term got applied, although we have no proof of either activity or the lack thereof.

Vladimir de Pachmann: Precursor to Glenn Gould who muttered and sang to himself and talked to the audience whilst playing. Said milking cows was the best finger/hand exercize and wore a tattered bathrobe he said was Chopin's. Somehow I think if Chopin bought a NEW pair of white gloves every single day of his life, I don't think he would have worn a tattered bathrobe or certainly wouldn't have given it to de Pachmann. Besides, their dates don't match.

Vladimir Horowitz: Married Wanda Toscanini

Wagner: Mark Twain said "Wagner's music is better than it sounds."

Yang ch'in: Translation is "foreign zither" – see Zither or see Dulcimer or see Psaltery or any Chinese herbalist.

Zither: This is, in actual fact, an instrument, but it's here mainly to fill out the Z's, as there usually aren't many entries here. It's a flat wooden soundbox with 30 to 45 strings. The four or five melody strings are plucked with a plectrum and the rest are plucked by fingers. The difference between being plucked by a plectrum and being plucked by bare fingers is an exhilarating experience that matches few others I've known (and I've known quite a few!).

Appendix B: Excerpts from the "Dear Anthon" piano advice column in the Chezlee Sez (including beefs)

Dear Anthon,
I know the world thinks the Broadway musical composer Stephen Sondheim is the bee's knees. However, frequently, when I am attempting to play the piano accompaniment to one of his vocal pieces, I simply do not have enough thumbs and fingers to play all the notes facing me. What's going on here? Does Sondheim have extra digits? Or what?

Frustachea Vye

Dear Frustrachea,
Because Sondheim was born rich he doesn't care. Also he writes what really are notes for an orchestral score so that sometimes when you look at a 15-note chord, he's indicating the notes the whole damn orchestra is going to play. He also avoids commercial success with his music by deliberately adding the odd note here and there, just so it won't become a hit. Not that he's not brilliant: he is unquestionably. And he KNOWS what he's doing, unlike some three-syllabled English composers who don't deserve the name (but they're even richer!) So Anthon simply sends his sympatico vibes to you, Frustachea, and advises you to "JUST HIT AS MANY AS YOU CAN AND FORGET THE REST.

Anthon E. Darling

Dear Anthon,
I have accompanied a lot of singers in Benjamin Britten song cycles and it is my personal conclusion that the publisher made a major boo-boo and the accompaniments are OFF BY ONE! By that, I mean that the accompaniment for song 7 is really the accompaniment for song 6 and if you moved them all back one song, everything would work out much better. Could you comment on my hypothesis? Am I off the wall or what?

Dear Off the wall ...
You're absolutely right!

Anthon E Darling

Dear Anthon,

As a fellow piano instructor, I must say how much I enjoy your column in the *Chezlee Sez*. It is a weekly ray of sunshine that illuminates the darkness of my 73 hours a week of giving private piano lessons. Financial impecunity forces me to have such a heavy load, but you do lighten it and I look forward to meeting you in the near future.

My question is simple. How do you get a student to play MUSICALLY? or does it just come naturally? So many of my little dears play like wooden typists. I find it particularly difficult when working with the pre-pubescent, pubescent and post-pubescent males to get them to "express" themselves. Can you enlighten me? I await your response eagerly.

An anguished cry from a peer,

Miss N.G. Pucock, B.N.

Dear "...cry from a peer,"

I'm so glad you've asked this question! I've been wanting to write about it for some time! There are dangers and I shall relate them to you in all honesty, Miss N.G. Pucock, because I feel one must be open to all truth no matter how hurtful.

1. DRAW THEM A MAP

This is what I call the piggyback method that I use when faced with the "robot" player who might as well be using an Olivetti Underwood. Go through the piece. Point out each and every nuance. Faster here. Louder here. Slow down right here. Tease them here. Etc. etc. etc. My hope is that, like learning to ride a bicycle, they will one day just "take over" and start doing it themselves, having learned the principles from the specifics that you've been giving them. This method doesn't always work, as the "learned" expression can become just as wooden as the way they played before and one also has to realize that some of the little buggers just ain't got no feeling no how and they're never going to "get it," so they're better to take up macramé or floor polishing.

2 LIFE EXPERIENCES

Encourage them to have "life experiences" that they can then incorporate into their music. That method, however, is fraught with many dangerous risks, some of which I myself have suffered.

I remember telling the Hungstraff boy to "get out there and live, boy! LIVE!" after falling asleep 13 times during a movement of a Kuhlau sonatina. Well, the Hungstraff boy did! He disappeared for three days while he was "living it up" and the young girl he was living it up with always said that at the climatic moment, he shouted, "For Anthon and for Brahms." She and her mother have always been a bit crisp and brusque with all of us here in Obscuria and she, as a result of the Hungstraff boy's "search for life," stopped studying with me. Her mother takes her to the east side of town for piano lessons with Cyril Crouch, an obviously inferior piano instructor to moi!

The other incident that resulted from my encouraging an adolescent to "live! live! live!" did involve illegal substances and a brief encounter with the local constabulary. But you know, after that, the little bugger played with such impassioned fervor I seriously thought about adopting it as a teaching method with Saturday evening soirées for special students! However, Constable Brown was quite explicit as to the possible consequences of such adventures, so I reverted to the piggyback method.

So, in short, which really is no longer applicable, do what you can but sometimes you just have to wait and let Mother Nature take her course and sometimes she hits them so hard that "feeling" a Brahms intermezzo takes a secondary if not tertiary place to "feeling" other things much more tangible than bar 54 of the Schubert *Impromptu* – which, to my mind, is a lot more exciting than what those little buggers are feeling.

Anyway, they soon quit piano and move on to other things far less interesting than Scarlatti and Scriabin and barely recognize you at the Feed Store when you're next there.

Good luck regardless, Miss N.G., and know that you always have a sympathetic ear hear dear.

Anthon E. Darling

Dear Anthon,

I have heard you speak oft about that Mrs. Robert Schumann and her condemning all of us to a life of LIVING HELL having to MEMORIZE every damn piece we play. However, given that that IS the STATUS QUO, do you have any memorizing hints or suggestions? I have a memory like a sieve and halfway through a piece longer than a page, I lose it and have to start all over again from the beginning, which is really embarrassing at recitals and does not earn you extra marks at the exam.

Can you help the helpless?

Forgettable, in every way

Dear Forgettable

I'm going to come straight to the point and tell you there are four ways to memorize a piece of music, and they are:

1. DIGITAL

You practise the piece SO MUCH that your fingers remember the patterns and once you've started them off they just keep going. The performance of the piece needs to be much more, but as a basis for remembering, the digital method of practise, practise, practise is at least something you can DO SOMETHING ABOUT – i.e. practise, practise, practise. This method is based on the principle that "your body remembers EVERYTHING it's ever done!!!" I personally find this a little scary a concept considering some of the things my body's been through in my lifetime. However, the "primal screamers" of the '70s when they did their primal screaming did go into the breach position to do their "birth screaming" if they had been breach birthed, so I guess it's a valid supposition. In spite of all that, digital memory is at least something that you can work at.

2. AURAL

This is partly a GIFT. Some people play totally by ear, don't need a note of music, but hear in their head and can put into their fingers entire pieces of music. Others are tone deaf and can't tell the difference between *Für Elise* and a fox in the hen house. The rest of us lie somewhere in between. Knowing by EAR (aurally) where the next note is helps if you're looking for it on the keyboard. I myself do NOT "play by ear" but my ear does remember what the next note or notes should be, so that helps.

3. VISUAL

Some people *see* the entire written score of the music in their mind's eye. This is called a photographic memory and these people just blissfully read "the music in their minds" and never have to worry. The rest of us are somewhere below that and – like me, for instance – know exactly where on the page that next chord is, if only I could "see" the actual notes that make up the damn chord, I could play it. For larger pieces it does help if you know that the first movement ends at the bottom of the third page, L.H. side, and the second movement – a scherzo – starts at the top of R.H. page 4. Visualization helps and you can, through practice, work at improving it.

4. STRUCTURAL

Like DIGITAL memory, this is something you can and SHOULD do something about. You can analyze the form and structure, know the key(s) and cadence, where phrases end and start. In other words, ANALYZE whatever it is that your playing to the nth degree. You should ALWAYS do this ANYWAY, not just if you're memorizing. You must *know* what it is you're playing when you play it. This structural knowledge is, of course, a great help to memorizing. As your fingers are whizzing over the keys, your thoughts might be going like this:

"...*tah-tuca-tuca-tuca-tah, pum-pum-peem-baaaaaaaaah* ... now I'm nearing the end of the EXPOSITION and I'm in the key of the Tonic ... and now ... the DEVELOPMENT ... and the first KEY I modulate into is ... B-flat major ... now B-flat minor ... and sequence sequence sequence and G minor ... then second theme ... to ..."

Do you see what I mean? The person thinking these kinds of thoughts is not going to get lost.

And last, en genéral, FOCUS. Focus intently and intensely on what you're doing. If while you fingers are flying or meandering over the keys, you are having thoughts like:

"...should I have rigatoni or linguini with the shrimp?

...I wonder if he/she's attached?

...next summer, I'm going further than Brampton

...I'd rather be whitewater rapid canoeing at Lake Wannalottapittee than here playing this ... oh my God ... what am I playing ...???? #%!$#@"

Do you see what I mean? Do you see what can happen if you lose your focus? So stay focused or you're up your Bach without a fugue.

Yours, Anthon

Appendix C **: A List of Yer Major Pee-an-ists!

LIST OF MAJOR PIANISTS!
(and if I've left your name out, I'm sorry. Please forgive me.
Ring me in Chezlee Ont and I'll add it to a supplement coming out
next year, maybe):

Oldies	*2 TOPS of the 20th Century*
Bach	Rubenstein
Mozart	Horowitz
Beethoven	*Canucks*
Chopin	Glenn Gould
Liszt	William Aide
Other 20th Century Greats	Oscar Peterson
Geza Anda	*CoolCats*
Martha Argerich	Rick Wakeman
Rudolph Serkin	Dave Brubeck
Solomon	Duke Ellington
Walter Gieseking	Liberace
Emil Gilels	Yanni
Claudio Arrau	Fats Waller
Vladimir Ashkinazy	*Chezlee*
Radu Lupu	Francine
Murray Perahia	Velma Spragge, Marvell Pye
Sviatoslav Richter	Jade Jones
Alfred Brendel	Yours Truly
Daniel Barenboim	
Alicia de Larrocha	
Others	*Additional*
Van Cliburn	Myra Hess
(could have been better	Cassadesus
if he'd ever left home)	Busoni
	De Pachnann

** I had mine out at T.G.H. It was the largest one on record. And
that's the truth.

A Call From Colli:
"I … ah … on a shlight …ah … detour…"

Just as I was putting the finishing touches on Appendix 3, late last Tuesday, the phone rang and Shirleen said it was a collect call from what sounded like a "Callee" and she had said "Are you the Collee or call-er" and the person on the other end had replied (not without expletives) "Get me Anthon or DIE!" and coughed and wheezed a lot.

Indeed it was our dear Colli Albani calling and he was not in good shape. The whole research project for S.W.A.P.S. on the subject of music and its effect on the dental area – titled "Teeth and Toccatas" had gone up in smoke, or, to be more literal, down the drain. Honest scholar that he is, Colli had discovered that there was indeed NO relationship whatsoever between the two. The head people at S.W.A.P.S. then accused him of fraudulent use of their funding, to which Colli replied "You asked ME here, I didn't ask you!" From there things went from bad to worse and the infamous Albani temper flared.

Even in a book as honest and open as this one is, I cannot go into the grisly details of what went on subsequently. Suffice it to say, Colli was calling me from a truck-stop road-side café and bar somewhere on a back road in Tennessee, where he'd hooked up with a lady biker by the name of Cindy-Sue and that night they were planning to wed and establish a free-thinking community somewhere in the Dakotas, North or South.

Colli does take criticism rather badly and questioning of his integrity does tend to drive him to the nearest watering hole for consolation.

He was very consoled when he called and I can only hope and pray that Cindy-Sue will read his name and address that I sewed into the back of his BVDs and mail him home. I'd even pay C.O.D.

I do miss the stimulation that the presence of his mind gives me and I do trust that his absence during the writing of this current tome, both physically and intellectually, has in no way affected the efficiency and poignancy of the points to be made, the comprehensiveness of the coverage, or the general scholarly and collegial level of the work. I do owe him so much and honestly, valiant reader to the bitter end, I'm a bit worried if he'll ever come back to Obscuria again. There was such bitterness filtering through the bourbon on the phone last Tuesday, it's unsettled me. And if that two-bit Tennessee floozy kidnaps him to the Dakotas, I don't know what I'd do ...

It's Ripple time and I only have one little bit left so I'm off to the Ox & Udder.

A Nocturnal Musette:
"...reflecting on the 88 at dusk!"

In actual fact that should more accurately read "reflections under the 88," as I am currently lying under the Petrof grand piano that we rented for the Four Square Gospel Hall Annual Parsnip and Arts Festival Competition. Last night were the semi-finals and both my students did not make it IN SPITE OF the fact that their piano playing was far superior to the thumping and grinding of the two who won — both pupils of thee Miss P.Q. Lunchley — and YES I'm naming her. Imagine! Inviting the out-of-town examiner to your own home for gooseberry surprise desserts and service-berry wine. God knows what time he got back to his hotel. I can't stand that kind of pandering after favoritism. It's immoral and I still don't know why he didn't thank me for the pound and a half of Lucetta's rutabaga chips that I left for him with the hotel desk clerk, Cyril. (Unless Cyril ate them himself, because he has been getting more *zaftig* lately.)

I'm sorry I've gotten off on this personal jag, but there is a point to be made here and I'm about to make it.

Shocking and sad as it is, the PIANO WORLD can be BIT-TER and ransacked with favoritism and unfairness, just like politics, baseball, and some of the other arts as well.

How this beautiful instrument that I am currently look-ing up under at as I lie here on the floor of the F.S.G.H. could get itself involved in the sordidity of human peccadilloes is beyong me. But even the ethereal beauty of the Brahms *Inter-mezzo Op. 117 No 2* or the spiritual depth of Bach's *Prelude and Fugue No 23* from *Book I* can be sullied, betimes, by human influence.

As well as being under the piano, I am also a bit under "the influence," as it were, as I was so bitter about that per-sonal loss in the semi-finals that after consoling my two stu-dents, assuring them that they had done well, I went straight to table 15 (at the back) of the O. & U. to seek solace. I must have sought a lot of solace as I'm not quite sure how I ended up here on the floor of the F.S.G.H ...

But as I think about it all ... from the point of view of the larger picture ... I can only make the following points, brusquely summed up as my head's not just right and I think dawn is approaching as I hear birds:

1. There ain't nothin' like music.
2. The piano's the best there is 'cause you can get it all with it.
3. A solo piano recital sure beats a solo bass clarinet re-cital!
4. Lucetta's rutabaga chips are better than Miss Lunchley's service-berry wine, anyday!
5. Piano music is a far better comforter than Stoney Ripple and doesn't leave you "under" the Petrof *and* the weather.
6. I've got to go now as I don't feel well ...

P.S. If anybody hears from Colli, tell the bugger to call me – collect if he wants to – as Lucetta and I and the sows, espe-cially Louise, do miss him ...

Index

About the Author

David E. Walden is currently an Associate Professor of Music at the Theatre School of Ryerson Polytechnic University in Toronto. He is now, primarily, a fuddy-duddy, absent-minded academe who writes and composes and is now rarely seen on the public stage, the TV screen or on film. All of which he has been seen on in the past. He was the original Old Deuteronomy in the Canadian production of *CATS*, Mr. Dressup's next-door-neighbor Dr. Miredo, a director in David Cronen- berg's *Dead Ringers*, etc., etc.

With Greg Finnegan he has written the music for a number of shows – one of which – *The Case of The Curious Cabaret* – has been produced successfully twice and the rest are soon to become international hits. He's written 100's of educational songs for kids, tons of music theatre songs that he's performed in shows with his friend Arlene Meadows and his cousin Howard Baer, and copious amounts of sacred works, pieces for piano and other works too numerous to mention. Lately he's gone deadly serious and written a REQUIEM IN REMEMBRANCE OF THE GENOCIDES OF THE 20TH CENTURY as well as an autobiographical work call *Another Walden's Pond* soon to be published.

A 'jack of all trades' and 'master of one' he continues to proliferate his work indiscriminately upon the unsuspecting public, never being able to be completely serious about anything, but never able to shake off the"teacher" side which he has also exercized his entire life. He says he's a hundred and six and at times.... !

About the Cartoonist

Mike Duncan is a successful non-graduate of both Sheridan College and Brock University. After a nine-year stint in commercial radio, only to rejoin radio again, he boldly decided to join the noble ranks of freelance illustration. An example for his generation, Mike Duncan has been hailed as of the nation's great underachievers. As for his future, give him a call.

Other books by David E. Walden:

How to Stay Awake
During Anybody's Second Movement
by David E. Walden, cartoons Mike Duncan
preface by Charlie Farquharson
isbn 0-920151-20-5

How To Listen To Modern Music
Without Earplugs
by David E. Walden, cartoons by Mike Duncan
foreword Bramwell Tovey
isbn 0-920151-31-0

Music Theory for the Bored and Confused
illustrations by Linda Nicholson
Published by Berandol Music

Music Theory for the Bored and Confused Book II
illustrations by Linda Nicholson
Published by Berandol Music

Understanding the Language of Music
Book I, II & III
Published by Berandol Music

with Lois Birkenshaw-Fleming
The Goat with the Bright Red Socks
(illustrations by Tach Bui)
Published by Berandol Music

Other forthcoming books from Prof. Darling's Prolific Pen:

Albinoni to Zittersdorf and Bach Again
Professor Anthon E. Darling, B.S.'s Guide to Composers
Living and/or Dead

Thee Opera
*Prof. Darling Shares His Many Opinions on this Art Form,
with Specific Reference to Special-Needs Groups such as
Wagner*

The Bagpipes: Musical Instrument or Lethal Weapon?
*A controversial look at one of the world's most
provocative sounds*

Other Sound And Vision books by David W. Barber,
with cartoons by Dave Donald:

A Musician's Dictionary
preface by Yehudi Menuhin
isbn 0-920151-21-3

Bach, Beethoven and the Boys
Music History as It Ought to Be Taught
preface by Anthony Burgess
isbn 0-920151-10-8

When the Fat Lady Sings
Opera History as It Ought to Be Taught
preface by Maureen Forrester
foreword by Anna Russell
isbn 0-920151-34-5

If it Ain't Baroque
More Music History as It Ought to Be Taught
isbn 0-920151-15-9

Getting a Handel on Messiah
preface by Trevor Pinnock
isbn 0-920151-17-5

Tenors, Tantrums and Trills
An Opera Dictionary from Aida to Zzzz
isbn 0-920151-19-1

TuTus, Tights and Tiptoes
Ballet History as It Ought to Be Taught
preface by Karen Kain
isbn 0-920151-30-2

by David W. Barber: (Editor)
Better Than It Sounds
A Dictionary of Humorous Musical Quotations
isbn 0-920151-22-1

The Last Laugh
Essays and Oddities in the News
preface by Ben Wicks
isbn 0-920151-94-9

Other musical humor books from Sound And Vision:

The Composers
A Hystery of Music
by Kevin Reeves
preface by Daniel Taylor
isbn 0-920151-29-9

1812 And all That
A Consise History of Music from 30.000 BC to the Millennium
by Lawrence Leonard, cartoons Emma Bebbington
isbn 0-920151-33-7

Opera Antics & Annecdotes
by Stephen Tanner, cartoons Umberto Tàcola
preface David W. Barber
isbn 0-920151-32-9

Love Lives of the Great Composers
From Gesualdo to Wagner
by Basil Howitt
isbn 0-920151-18-3

A Working Musician's Joke Book
by Daniel G. Theaker, cartoons by Mike Freen
preface David W. Barber
isbn 0-920151-23-X

I Wanna Be Sedated
Pop Music in the Seventies
by Phil Dellio & Scott Woods, cartoons Dave Prothero
preface Chuck Eddy
isbn 0-920151-16-7

Quotable Pop
Fifty Decades of Blah Blah Blah
A Quotable Press Book
by Phil Dellio & Scott Woods, cartoons Mike Routh
isbn 0-920151-50-7

Quotable Alice
A Quotable Press Book
by David W. Barber
isbn 0-920151-52-3

Quotable Sherlock
A Quotable Press Book
by David W. Barber
isbn 0-920151-53-1

The Thing I've Played With The Most
@ David E. Walden, 2000
@ Mike Duncan [Cartoons] 2000

First published in Canada by
Sound And Vision
359 Riverdale Avenue
Toronto, Canada M4J 1A4

http://www.soundandvision.com
E-mail: musicbooks@soundandvision.com

First printing, March 2001
1 3 5 7 9 11 13 15 - printings - 14 12 10 8 6 4 2

Canadian Cataloguing in Publication Data

Walden, David E
the thing I've played with the most
Includes index
ISBN 0-920151-35-3
1. Music – History and criticism – Humor. I. Title
ML160L582 2000   780'.207   C00-931811-9

Jacket design by Jim Stubbington

Typeset in Century Schoolbook
Printed and bound in Canada
by Agmv Marquis, Quebec

Note from the Publisher

Sound And Vision books may be purchased for educational or promotional use or for special sales. If you have any comments on this book or any other books we publish, or if you would like a catalogue, please write to us at Sound And Vision 359 Riverdale Avenue, Toronto, Canada M4J1A4.

Or visit our web site at http://www.soundandvision. com.

We are always looking for original books to publish. If you have an idea or manuscript that is in the genre of musical humour including educational themes, please contact us. Thank you for purchasing or borrowing this book.

Geoffrey Savage
Publisher